BIPOLAR II AND THE BLACK WOMAN

A Guide to Wellness for African Americans

APRIL S. LILY

Disclaimer Notice:

Please note the information contained within this document is for educational and entertainment purposes only. All effort has been executed to present accurate, up-to-date, and reliable, complete information. No warranties of any kind are declared or implied. Readers acknowledge that the author is not engaging in the rendering of legal, financial, medical, or professional advice. The content within this book has been derived from various sources. Please consult a licensed professional before attempting any techniques outlined in this book. By reading this document, the reader agrees that under no circumstances is the author responsible for any losses, direct or indirect, which are incurred as a result of the use of the information contained within this document, including, but not limited to, — errors, omissions, or inaccuracies.

TABLE OF CONTENTS

- ❖ INTRODUCTION
- ❖ WHAT IS BIPOLAR DISORDER?
- ❖ TYPES OF BIPOLAR DISORDER
- ❖ HOW BIPOLAR II AFFECTS BLACK WOMEN
- ❖ BIPOLAR SYMPTIOMS IN BLACK WOMEN
- ❖ BIPOLAR II IN BLACK WOMEN: CULTURAL AND SOCIETAL FACTORS
- ❖ BIPOLAR II IMPACT ON BLACK WOMEN
- ❖ BIPOLAR II EMOTIONAL TOLL ON BLACK WOMEN
- ❖ DIFFERENT KINDS OF DEPRESSION
- ❖ HOW STRONG IS YOUR DEPRESSION?
- ❖ MANIA AND HYPOMANIA
- ❖ BIPOLAR DISORDER ADAPTING
- ❖ CAUSES AND TRIGGERS
- ❖ MANAGING WARNING SYMPTOMS OF HYPOMANIA OR MANIA
- ❖ PSYCHOTHERAPHY
- ❖ SUPPORT AND ACTIVITY STRATEGIES TO RELIEVE DEPRESSION
- ❖ REDUCING SUICIDE RISK FOR BLACK WOMEN
- ❖ LIVING WELL

❖ CONCLUSION

❖ REFERENCE

INTRODUCTION

Biplar II and the Black Woman provides practical information on managing bipolar disorder to people and their families, friends, and partners. People with bipolar disorder, like me, who are part of a treatment program request more information on their condition and treatment. We need information that could combine the most recent research with practical, real-world advice relevant to our everyday lives. We request this information for our benefit and for those we care about to understand the bipolar disorder better and find solutions. I have gathered this information from clinical experience, current research, and the experiences of people living with bipolar disorder.

Bipolar disorder is also known as manic depression. However, they are not your typical mood swings. Bipolar disorder is more than just experiencing normal mood swings. You may also experience extreme highs or lows that seem independent of the events around you. These mood states can vary from very mild to severe at times. There may be a combination of low and high moods. These mood swings are caused by biological changes in brain areas that control mood. Bipolar disorder can be treated with medication. Bipolar disorder is not a temporary condition that disappears when you feel better. As with asthma—people living with asthma experience frequent attacks and different levels of wellness. Bipolar disorder attacks are very personal. These 'attacks' can cause changes in your mood, emotions, and behavior. These changes can have severe consequences for your safety and impact your finances, career, and relationships.

There are effective treatments and personal strategies to manage episodes and prevent relapse.

This book contains information on bipolar disorder, including its causes and triggers. It also includes treatment options. I provide information about ways to prevent relapses, minimize negative consequences, and deal with the effects of the illness. However, everyone finds a way to cope with their condition, but not all strategies work. This book outlines some common pitfalls that can make your illness worse or unhelpful and provides strategies that can help. We discuss ways to keep your bipolar disorder under control, how to make healthy lifestyle choices, and how to create your relapse prevention plan. This information can be combined with your personal experience to help you discover new ways to manage your illness or confirm your existing successful strategies.

It is important not to minimize the suffering and other negative effects caused by bipolar disorder. Bipolar disorder has also been linked to creativity, success, and fame. Bipolar disorder, despite its widespread prevalence, is still not fully understood. People living with bipolar disorder are often faced with additional difficulties. Unlike other illnesses like asthma, bipolar disorder comes with the stigma of "mental illness," which is harder to accept. We will discuss how to come to terms with your illness and live beyond the boundaries of stigma.

It may take some time to create a fulfilling life that helps you stay well. You may experience relapses at times. It is helpful to be prepared. This book will help you understand the illness and offer practical solutions. Management of bipolar disorder is part of living a full life. This book hopefully will help you to find inspiration and ideas.

WHAT IS BIPOLAR DISORDER?

Bipolar disorder was finally diagnosed. This meant that the moods had a name, and there is something we can do to control them. Although it did not reflect my entire experience or the effects bipolar disorder had upon my life, this name provided some explanation and a path forward.

Bipolar disorder is characterized by biological mood changes that are more severe, persistent, frequent, and disruptive than normal ups and downs. Recognizing the difficulty and burdens people suffering from bipolar disorder face, the search for a common language was intensified to describe and treat it. They have been divided into categories to make it easier for patients and doctors to diagnose, treat and understand the typical mood swings that can occur with bipolar disorder. This chapter will discuss the current classification for bipolar disorder. Bipolar disorder affects people differently, depending on how they experience it and how much their lives are affected.

These principles can be applied to your own experiences and may help you manage your illness.

It's important to recognize symptoms of other disorders such as anxiety and drug abuse that could be contributing to your distress. The current diagnosis system for bipolar disorder will likely be improved to include milder symptoms and account for overlaps with other mood disorders.

A LITTLE HISTORY

Bipolar disorder isn't a new disease. People knew about melancholia (depression) and mania in ancient Greece. Jean-Pierre Falret, a French psychiatrist, described the bipolar disorder as *la folie circulaire*. This condition involves changes from mania and melancholia. Jules Baillarger, a neurologist, explained these changes in 1854 as two stages of the same illness (folie a second form). Emil Kraepelin, a German psychiatrist, distinguished schizophrenia (characterized by psychotic symptoms like delusions and hallucinations, but not the extreme mood symptoms) from manic depression. In 1979, Karl Leonhard distinguished bipolar disorder and unipolar depression. Unipolar depression is depression that has no mania or hypomania.

BIPOLAR DISORDER DIAGNOSIS

Bipolar disorder is not a physical illness like stroke or diabetes. It cannot be diagnosed with a medical test, such as a brain scan or blood test. Diagnosis is based on the identification of your past and current symptoms. The Diagnostic and Statistical Manual of Mental Disorders (American Psychiatric Association 2000) and the International Classification of Diseases (ICD-10)

The 2006 World Health Organisation guidelines for diagnosing certain conditions.

The illness typically begins in the teen years or early twenties. However, it can also occur later or earlier in life. Many people have reported that their bipolar disorder was not diagnosed quickly, and they had to wait a while before being treated.

Episodes of illness

Bipolar disorder is characterized by 'episodes of illness.' To be diagnosed with bipolar disorder, you must have had an episode of mania, hypomania, or mixed episode at some point in your life. Depressive episodes are common, but milder forms can also occur. These episodes can be severe or mild, depending on whether you are severely ill or have a series of symptoms. Although the likelihood of experiencing another bout of bipolar disorder is high, ongoing treatment can help prevent relapse.

An episode of major depression

When you feel depressed, it is called a depressive episode. Symptoms last at least two weeks and cause distress in your daily life, relationships, work, or work relationships. An episode of depression can be diagnosed if you have five or greater symptoms. These symptoms include:

- Depressed mood may be characterized by intense sadness, emptiness or tearfulness, and irritability.

- A loss of interest in or enjoyment in something that lasts almost all day.

  Other possible symptoms include:

- Insufficiency of energy and chronic tiredness.

- Restlessness, lethargy, or a marked lack of activity.

- Noticeable changes in appetite or weight (up or down).

- Sleep problems can include difficulty falling asleep, difficulty waking up during the night, being unable or unwilling to go back to sleep, and sleeping too much.

- Feelings of worthlessness or excessive guilt.

- Having trouble concentrating, poor memory, or difficulty making decisions.

- Persistent thoughts about suicide, death, or hopelessness.

  People can experience psychotic symptoms along with their depression. These symptoms can include hallucinations and delusions, which are strong beliefs that don't connect with reality.

A case of Mania

A DSM-IV classification defines mania as an "episode of mania."

If your mood is extreme, high, or irritable for more than a week, you could be manic. You must have at least three of the following symptoms (four if your mood is irritable).

- You feel that you need less sleep than you used to.

- Your thoughts can race so fast that it is easy to get lost and find it hard to express your ideas.

- Talking more than usual or feeling pressure to continue talking.

- Being easily distracted from important tasks to attend to unimportant or irrelevant things.

- Feeling a significant increase in self-esteem or feeling that you have special gifts or talents you don't have.

- Increased activity to achieve goals (at school, work, or sexually) and increased restlessness or agitation

- Exercising in pleasure activities without regard to the consequences such as gambling, huge buying sprees, irresponsible investment, high sex drive, and sexual indiscretions.

Mania is diagnosed if these symptoms cause severe disruptions to your work or social life. Mania, like depression, may also include psychotic symptoms such as hallucinations or delusions related to your mood. Mania can also have extremely disordered and confused thinking.

Hypomania

Hypomania can be diagnosed using similar symptoms.

Hypomania is similar to mania, but it's milder and shorter. These symptoms aren't necessarily disruptive, and you might be able to continue your daily activities. However, others will notice changes in your behavior. Hypomania must last at least four days before it can be considered. Hypomania does not involve psychotic symptoms.

Mixed episodes

You can experience the highs and lows. However, many people experience both. This is like experiencing hot and cold, or even black and white simultaneously. It is possible to experience both mania and depression simultaneously. This combination can have specific implications for your treatment. It is important to recognize it.

For at least one week, the symptoms cause substantial disruption to your everyday life, sometimes necessitating hospitalization. You may experience rapid mood swings (happy, sad, or irritable), less sleep, decreased appetite, restlessness, risky activities, and delusions of unrealistic guilt.

Some other classifications of mixed state do not require you to have both manic and depressive episodes simultaneously. People who are depressed may experience a few symptoms such as racing thoughts or restlessness, or people who are manic may have isolated symptoms like depression, irritability, or suicidal thinking. Depending on the symptoms, mixed states can be classified into manic and depressive states.

Some people are more prone to mixed states, but illicit drug use could play a part in developing diverse forms. Certain antidepressants may exacerbate varied conditions.

People with mixed states are more susceptible to psychotic symptoms, such as paranoid thoughts or hearing voices.

TYPES BIPOLAR DISORDER

People with bipolar disorder can experience different episodes. Bipolar I and II disorders are the dominant patterns as outlined by DSM-IV. Other categories include cyclothymic disorder and bipolar disorder not yet specified (NOS). These patterns can be associated with or without psychotic symptoms or rapid cycling. Many symptoms can be severe. Some may even occur in the same person for a long time.

BIPOLAR I

Manic episodes can occur with or without depressive symptoms in this type of bipolar disorder. This type of bipolar disorder can cause manic episodes that last up to a week. You may need to be admitted to the hospital if your mania is severe. You don't necessarily have depression to be diagnosed with Bipolar I. However, you may experience depression lasting more than two weeks.

BIPOLAR II

Bipolar II disorder can be described as having manic episodes and depressive episodes. This type of mania is less severe than Bipolar I, so it's called Hypomania. Bipolar II can cause major depressive episodes before or after a manic episode.

CYCLOTHYMIC DISORDER

Cyclothymic disorder is characterized by depressive and manic episodes lasting for at least two years. The same applies to children. However, they must experience both manic and depressive episodes for at least one year before being diagnosed. This disorder is usually less severe than Bipolar I and Bipolar II. The cyclothymic disease can cause unstable moods. You may experience periods of normalcy with depression and mania.

OTHER TYPES

Some symptoms may not be consistent with the three other bipolar types. You may have type IV or "other" bipolar symptoms. This could be due to drugs, alcohol, and underlying medical conditions.

Bipolar Disorder NOS can be used to diagnose episodes of illness that don't last long enough to be classified as hypomanic or mixed depressive episodes or do not present with the required number of symptoms.

Bipolar Disorder NOS is a term that refers to temperaments. It also allows us to subdivide bipolar disorders further along a continuum, from the more severe to the milder forms. Some people might have mild bipolar symptoms that sometimes develop into more severe forms of bipolar disorder.

- **Hyperthymic:** Very cheerful, optimistic, and confident.

- **Cyclothymic:** Changing levels of self-esteem and mood swings.

- **Dysthymic**: Usually joyless and lacking energy, but not as severe depression.

- **Mixed:** Mild symptoms of anxiety, restlessness, sadness, and irritability.

The bipolar spectrum

A diagnosis of the unipolar disorder may be possible for people who have not experienced hypomania or mania. Bipolar disorder is often seen as distinct from unipolar disorder. The difference between bipolar disorder and unipolar disorder is not so clear-cut. You may experience mild to moderate mood elevations, but not enough to make you suspect that you have bipolar disorder. You may be able to benefit from treatment for bipolar disorder if you have these symptoms. Hypomania can also occur in people with unipolar depression.

Although this spectrum's boundaries are unclear, nearly half of those with depression are probably affected by bipolar disorder. Bipolar disorder patients are more likely than others to suffer from depression associated with sleep disturbances and fatigue. They also tend to have a greater chance of experiencing feelings of sadness and flatness.

❖ RAPID CYCLING

It is cycling when you go from one episode, such as depression, to another, such as mania or mixed states. Rapid cycling is having at least four episodes of mania or depression in a given year. However, some people can cycle within days or weeks. Rapid cycling is common in people with bipolar disorder, with around 15% to 25% of them experiencing it. Rapid cycling is a different treatment for people who do not have it. It is important to recognize if you have this pattern.

Rapid cycling is more common in women and younger people. They are also more likely to have been diagnosed later in life and had more hospitalizations and episodes. Thyroid problems or antidepressants may cause rapid cycling. Some people experience depression as their dominant experience, even though they may go through periods of depression and mania.

❖ SEASONAL PATTERN

Some people notice that they have more episodes during certain times of the year. You may experience a major depressive episode during winter or autumn and a hypomanic/manic episode during spring or summer. These patterns can help you prevent or reduce your episode's severity.

To get the correct treatment, the bipolar disorder must be distinguished from symptoms and signs that may resemble it. Bipolar disorder is not all mood swings. Many people experience worse or better days. The ups or downs of life can sometimes trigger these mood swings. Bipolar disorder is not likely to cause mood swings that aren't out of the ordinary, like those that are normal and understandable or that aren't distressing, disruptive, or visible. Bipolar disorder is distinguished from unipolar depression by hypomanic, manic, or mixed episodes. Bipolar disorder is sometimes confused with schizophrenia and other illnesses that are psychotic. Schizophrenia is characterized by periods of severe psychotic symptoms such as delusions, hallucinations, and disordered thoughts. However, schizophrenia is not associated with intense mood swings. People with schizophrenia can become depressed, but their psychotic symptoms don't occur without a manic episode.

Bipolar disorder is sometimes confused with schizoaffective, which can include mood and psychotic symptoms. Bipolar disorder has psychotic symptoms that are only present when there are mood symptoms. Schizoaffective disease, on the other hand, can cause psychotic symptoms when mood symptoms are absent for more than two weeks.

Borderline personality disorder can cause mood swings, although they are less common and last longer than that in bipolar disorder. Marginal personality mood swings result from events and are tied to a specific personality characteristic.

Although some altered states may be symptomatic of bipolar disorder, the effects of illicit drug use can quickly wear off and not cause permanent symptoms. Bipolar disorder can also be mimicked by symptoms such as multiple sclerosis or hypothyroidism. It is important to diagnose bipolar disorder correctly to provide the best treatment accurately.

❖ COMORBIDITY

Bipolar disorder may be present in combination with other conditions. You might also have other symptoms. This is known as comorbidity. Bipolar disorder can lead to anxiety and drug and alcohol problems.

Problems with alcohol and drugs

Some people with bipolar disorder don't have drug or alcohol problems. However, many people (50-70% of those with bipolar disorder) find their lives complicated by these extra difficulties (Brady & Sonne 1995). The most commonly used substance is alcohol. However, there are high levels of heroin, cocaine, amphetamines, benzodiazepine, and marijuana use in bipolar disorder patients. People with bipolar disorder are more likely to experience relapses, rapid cycling, suicide, and violent behavior (Balazs and colleagues, 2006). Therefore, people who suffer from drug and alcohol problems often have more severe symptoms, are hospitalized more frequently, and live with more disruption than those who don't abuse these substances.

Your bipolar disorder and life can be greatly improved if you are open to discussing your drug and alcohol issues. Sometimes it can be difficult to stop using drugs or alcohol, even if they know it is causing serious problems.

Anxiety

Anxiety is a common symptom of bipolar disorder. It may be more prevalent in Bipolar II disorder sufferers and Bipolar III disorder patients. Anxiety can be pre-existing to bipolar disorder. It may occur during an episode, as part of rapid cycling, or when you are feeling well. Anxiety can increase the chance of bipolar disorder recurrence for some people. Anxiety symptoms can be disorienting and distressing. People with bipolar disorder are increasingly conscious of the need for treatment and identification of their anxiety. Many people collaborate with their doctors to reduce their anxiety.

Anxiety can manifest as a range of symptoms, from mild symptoms to severe anxiety. It is important to distinguish between anxiety symptoms and symptoms of physical illness. These are some common anxiety symptoms:

- Increased heart rate, pounding, or palpitations
- Feeling short of breath or having a choking sensation
- Feeling dizzy, lightheaded, or disconnected from the world
- Shaking or trembling
- Concentration difficulties
- Nausea, vomiting, or diarrhea
- Pins and needles, or numbness
- Feeling very cold or hot flushes
- Aches and pains
- Indigestion
- Excessive worry
- Feelings of fear or dread and intense fear of losing control.

Anxiety disorders include panic disorder, specific anxiety, social anxiety, obsessive-compulsive disorder, post-traumatic stress disorder, generalized anxiety disorder, and social phobia. Talking to your doctor about your anxiety issues can help you get the best treatment.

Panic disorder without or with agoraphobia

Panic disorder refers to panic attacks that are brief and intense.

There are times when anxiety is a common condition. Agoraphobia is anxiety about being in unsafe situations. It can be avoided by staying away from your home or being around people. These situations can trigger panic attacks in some people.

❖ Certain phobias

Avoid specific phobias that cause excessive or irrational anxiety.

Specific objects or events, such as flying, spiders, or snakes.

❖ Social phobia

How others judge you in social situations will determine how you perform. You might avoid certain social problems and feel panicked or distressed about anticipating them.

Obsessive-compulsive disorder

Obsessions can be defined as persistent, intrusive thoughts or impulses that are persistent and dangerous.

These are difficult to ignore or stop but can cause distress. Compulsive actions are repeated actions that you do to relieve or prevent problems. These compulsions and obsessions can disrupt your day.

Post-traumatic stress disorder

Sometimes, post-traumatic stress disorder can occur after you have experienced a traumatic event.

A very frightening or traumatic event occurred that evoked fear and anxiety.

Extreme fear and helplessness. You may experience the event differently, such as flashbacks or nightmares. You may be able to avoid associations or reminders of the incident and thus, cut off any feelings. This can cause you to feel extremely distressed and may interfere with your daily activities.

Generalized anxiety disorder

Anxiety and excessive worry, combined with symptoms like difficulty concentrating, sleep disturbances, and feeling on edge, unsettled or tired, can lead to anxiety and panic attacks. Anxiety that lasts more than six months can make you feel anxious and disrupt your daily functioning.

Bipolar depression can be more than feeling blue from life's daily stresses and strains. Depression can be more severe, lasts longer than this, and can interfere with your everyday life. Your mood is a combination of your thoughts, feelings, and behavior, along with the biological changes in your brain. There are many ways to experience depression, depending on how severe they are, what combination you have, and how often. Recognizing your own experience signify that you are not the only one. Around 90% of those with bipolar disorder suffer from depression at one time or another. Depression can seem overwhelming and endless at times. However, there are many ways to manage it.

We will discuss this more in the following chapters. Depression is something you have. Depression isn't your fault, just as asthma or other illnesses are not your faults. Recognizing symptoms and your depression can help you identify and implement the best treatment strategies.

What Changes If You Are Depressed

Below are some of the mood, thinking, and behavior changes that people with bipolar depression report. These changes may have been experienced by you or someone close to you.

Feelings changed:

How you feel can change.

There is no emotion or crying.

Depression can cause people to feel empty and flat.

Some people think of constant sadness or tearfulness.

They no longer care about the things that once mattered to them.

Nothing is interesting

Sometimes you may lose motivation and interest in doing things. Sometimes, it is hard to find the cause.

Even if something is good, people won't feel any better.

You can't enjoy anything.

Your ability to feel pleasure may be reduced.

Many people notice a decrease in their sexual drive.

You may experience a reduction in your senses.

Even the smell and taste of things can be diminished, making them look greyer.

Too tired, no energy.

Many people who have bipolar disorder feel they are not getting enough sleep.

You may feel like you've just completed a marathon.

Have no energy left.

Mornings are worse.

It is possible to feel worse at certain times, particularly in the evenings.

Mornings feel bad, though some people feel worse at night.

Worthless

A fall in self-esteem is an important indicator.

They lack confidence, feel insignificant and forget their strengths and talents temporarily.

Guilt

For minor errors or careless mistakes, you may feel too guilty.

Rejection and criticism

People become more sensitive towards criticism and rejection.

Aggressive, impatient, irritable.

Intense, aggressive, argumentative, impatient, and irritable.

It is important to share your feelings with others when you are experiencing depression, mania, or mixed states.

Hopeless, helpless

You can also identify depression by the feeling of hopelessness.

You may feel anxious about the future and helpless about changing things. This hopelessness can lead to suicidal thoughts if it is severe.

Be anxious, be worried

This anxiety can also cause worry about other people.

Worrying about your physical health is impossible if you are focusing on something else.

Anxiety symptoms that manifest as physical symptoms.

Common anxiety symptoms include tremors, sweating, and racing thoughts, heartburn, cold or hot flushes, discomfort in the stomach, chest, or heart.

Aches and Pains

Many people feel many physical discomforts and pains.

An increase in physical symptoms or increased visits to the doctor for an otherwise healthy person could be a sign of depression.

Activity is low

There may be changes in your activities, including:

Hibernation

Depression has been likened to hibernation, a type of hibernation that occurs from the world. Even the most outgoing people can find it difficult to accept invitations when they feel depressed.

Lethargy

Lethargy is feeling tired, unmotivated, and slowing down.

Bipolar depression can cause people to speak slower, use shorter sentences, and move slowly. According to outsiders, people with depression may show fewer gestures or facial expressions. This decrease in activity can be milder and make it more difficult to stick to plans or get up in the morning. Sometimes thoughts can slow down and become less frequent. In its most severe form, lethargy can make it difficult to do basic tasks or get out of bed.

Agitation

People with depression may experience fever.

They may find it difficult to sit still or are restless.

Avoidance, withdrawal, and procrastination

Refusing to complete tasks or withdrawing commitments.

Growing depression can manifest in avoiding social contact and making many impulsive decisions.

Sleeping and eating

Depression can impact basic activities like sleeping and eating.

Bipolar depression is characterized by sleeping more than usual. However, some people with the disorder experience insomnia as a sign that they are hungry more.

Depression

You may find your thinking more negative and one-sided. Temporary memory and concentration problems can affect your sharpness and slow your review.

Negative Thinking

The voice of depression is often a bully and it tends to block other options. Depression tells you what you can't do, what we shouldn't do and how terrible things are. There are two basic orientations that we can take that will help control it. Insist on rational questioning and alternatives and basic compassion.

Even in a stable mood, it is normal to experience negative thoughts at times. But depression can also be seen as seeing yourself, others, and the future through a different lens.

A rigid approach is the most destructive and damaging.

One-sided, negative interpretations of events are often untrusting. For example, "I failed to pass this exam" could be applied to every situation. You may find your thinking dominated by negative thoughts from the past or worrying about the future. This can make it difficult to think about other things. This is known as 'rumination.' Both cognitive behavior therapy (CBT) and mindfulness-based psychotherapy (MBP) have strategies that have been proven to help deal with depressed thoughts.

Slow thoughts and poor memory

A big indicator of depression is the feeling that you feel like you are in a rut.

Your head is foggy. These strategies include temporarily lowering your expectations and setting smaller, more achievable goals.

HOW BIPOLAR II AFFECT BLACK WOMEN

Bipolar II disorder can affect many aspects of your life. Bipolar II symptoms can vary depending on the person. However, people, who have it experience both depressive and hypomanic episodes (less severe than the manic) that can cause them to feel high, active, and happy.

The media often overlook this type of bipolar disorder. They tend to focus on the more severe symptoms of Bipolar I disorder. This book will explore Bipolar II in black women. We know from experience that many black women are affected, but we don't know why. This dangerous condition is more common in black women than in white women. Black women are more likely stigmatized if they speak out about their bipolar disorder.

Bipolar disorders are more common in women than in men. However, the ratio of male to female bipolar disorder symptoms is 1:1. Women are more likely than men to experience depressive episodes.The research found that Bipolar II females had more manic episodes and fewer depressive episodes than those with Bipolar I. This could be because women are more likely to experience hypomanic episodes in Bipolar II than men. However, they have fewer depressive episodes. Blacks and whites with Bipolar Disorder II or I have the same number of manic-depressive attacks. Bipolar II subjects were more likely than others to be married or cohabited.

BIPOLAR II SYMPTOMS IN BLACK WOMEN

Bipolar II can cause anxiety, mood swings and depression, low self-esteem, and chronic fatigue. You can take control of your condition by learning about it and addressing it head-on.

Bipolar II is a mental disorder that can affect many people around the globe. The severity of the mental illness will influence how you experience symptoms. The National Institute of Mental Health (NIMH) defines Bipolar II as a mood disorder that severely affects the person's emotions, behavior, and self-image.

Bipolar II can be managed without the need for drastic measures. Many medications can be used to manage bipolar disorder. Most people with the condition live normal, productive lives. Many sufferers are not receiving the proper treatment because they are often misdiagnosed or undertreated for this mental illness.

One in three people living with bipolar disorder in the United States is not diagnosed. A black woman with bipolar disorder is often misdiagnosed as having depression or another mental illness. People with this disorder, or those who suspect it, should immediately seek treatment.

Bipolar II, which is less common than other bipolar disorders, affects less than one percent of adults in the United States, according to the National Institute of Mental Health.

Although symptoms of Bipolar II can look similar to depression, they are more severe and last for longer periods. Bipolar II refers to a woman who experiences mania or hypomania. These are times when she experiences grandiosity and irritability. Bipolar II is a term for a woman who has less severe symptoms.

A doctor will usually diagnose bipolar disorder by ruling any other causes out. The doctor may also check for other mental or physical conditions, family history, substance abuse, and medical history. The doctor will also examine the frequency and duration of the symptoms.

It can be difficult to determine if a woman is having a manic episode or just having a good day.

BIPOLAR II IN BLACK WOMEN: CULTURAL AND SOCIETAL FACTORS

Bipolar II disorder, a mood disorder that is often not recognized in black women, is often undiagnosed. Although it is less common than Bipolar I disorder, it can still be dangerous. It is easy to miss or misunderstand the symptoms, diagnosis, and treatment.

As with many cultural groups, people of African descent have a long history of mental illness. Many factors influence the prevalence of mental disorders in Africa. In some countries, such as Nigeria and Zimbabwe, 40% to 40% of the population may have a mental disorder. South Africa is the country with the highest prevalence of mental illness.

Numerous studies have been done to examine the mental health of Africans. One study in Zimbabwe found that 12% of females and 8% of males had mood disorders, compared to Europe's 6% and 3%, respectively

- The prevalence rate for bipolar disorder in African Americans is nearly twice that of whites, and it is higher than any other ethnicity in the United States.

- This is an interesting finding, considering the 2.7% prevalence of the bipolar disorder among whites.

- Many studies have found that African-American women are more likely to suffer from mood disorders and bipolar disorder than any other ethnic group in America. This shows the importance of studying cultural and social factors related to mental illness in black women. Blacks have been segregated from whites since the beginning. They were enslaved and forced to follow the master's instructions to survive. Enslaved Africans were brought to America, where they were forced to live as enslaved people on plantations. They had no choice about their jobs, movement, or thought of freedom.

- Blacks were raised in this country with many disadvantages throughout their development and are still discriminated against today.

BIPOLAR II'S IMPACT ON BLACK WOMEN

Bipolar disorder is something we've all heard of, but what does it have to do about black women? The answer is, unfortunately, "quite a bit!"

Simply put, research shows that Bipolar II is more common in black women than in white women. Experts continue to debate this issue.

Cultural differences in the way depression and other symptoms of mood disorders are interpreted could be a reason. People who openly discuss their mental health in African American culture are more likely to feel stigmatized or judged by others than they experience empathy.

Another reason could be the higher stress levels experienced by African American women. Many of the same factors can contribute to mental health problems in the community, such as poverty, discrimination, and unemployment.

Researchers have recently begun to study the impact of socioeconomic status on Bipolar II in African American women who aren't also Hispanic/Latina. This means that if you are black and not Hispanic/Latina, you may have a higher chance of developing Bipolar II than someone who lives in an economically stable area.

BIPOLAR II'S EMOTIONAL TOLL ON BLACK WOMEN

Bipolar II shares many symptoms with Bipolar I. Bipolar II can cause both manic and depressive episodes. However, unlike Bipolar I, people with it only have to experience one of the two. Bipolar II sufferers are sometimes misdiagnosed and dismissed because they don't have all the symptoms. Children are more difficult to diagnose because they have fewer behavioral differences than adults.

Although more research is needed, some studies suggest that bipolar disorder can be more common in women than in men. According to the National Institute of Mental Health's 2000 study, 15% of bipolar patients were married. This compares to 6% for male patients. This is not the same as Carolyn Sue Perry's figures. She stated that in her book, "The Emotional toll of Bipolar II On Black Women," she found that black women with Bipolar II were at least 25%.

Bipolar II can have many negative consequences. Bipolar II can cause women to have trouble finding jobs due to extreme mood swings.

As a matter that affects not only black women with Bipolar II but also their communities, the treatment of this condition has been brought up. Black women have been marginalized and excluded from mental health care because of racial discrimination and cultural stigma.

Although this is commonly attributed to the small number of cases diagnosed, it does not include those who have symptoms privately or don't seek help.

Recent reports have shown that people living with bipolar disorder from African American women are at high risk of suicide and death.

DEEP SADNESS

According to the National Institute of Mental Health, African-American women are more likely to suffer from serious mental illnesses such as major depression or bipolar disorder. A potentially life-threatening condition can have devastating effects on anyone, but this is particularly true for black women who are often unable to access the proper treatment.

This is a fact that can't be denied for many reasons. However, black women are 53% more likely to end up in the emergency room than white women because they cannot get the help they need. They are also half as likely to commit suicide.

Black women with severe psychiatric illnesses face many challenges. These include poverty, high unemployment, and poor access to quality healthcare. Many end up in a hospital with no means of escape. The country must address the problems surrounding Blacks' mental health so that it does not get worse.

Discrimination is a major reason for the high rates of mental illness in black women. Discrimination can cause depression. This can then lead to suicide attempts and suicidal thoughts among Blacks. The medical community should treat these women with compassion and understanding, not dismiss them as suffering from a mental illness.

Because of the skin color of black patients, mental health professionals can make misdiagnoses. Neglecting to treat women suffering from aggressive or psychotic symptoms can cause trauma and worsen the condition. Physicians can gain a deeper understanding of Black culture to help them be more culturally sensitive.

Black Women Suicide, Mental Health, And Stigma

Black women often face stereotypes about their sexuality, independence, and strength. Because mental health treatment is seen as a weakness, they are also subject to stigmas. Some people believe they can voice their opinions against racism but don't feel empowered to speak out against mental illness because of the stigma attached.

People with mental health problems may not seek treatment for many reasons. We will be discussing reasons beyond just being black. It's not just the stigma associated with being an black woman. Still, it's another factor black women have to deal with, in addition to the other effects of Bipolar II.

Suicide is a very serious issue in Black communities, and Bipolar II may be one of the contributing factors. Suicidal thoughts and attempts can be triggered by a lack of support or feeling isolated.

DIFFERENT KINDS DEPRESSION

There are many possible combinations or clusters of symptoms for depression, including atypical, psychotic, and mixed.

❖ Atypical depression

People with bipolar disorder may experience depression differently than those with unipolar depression. This is because the symptoms of bipolar disorder are not associated with hypomania or manic episodes. This is because this pattern can be called atypical instead of feeling sad or depressed, such as unipolar depression symptoms like insomnia and loss of appetite. People need to sleep more and eat less, and they feel more tired and slow down when depressed. Although you may temporarily feel better when things go well, this doesn't change the underlying cause of atypical depression (Cuellar et al., 2005).

❖ Psychotic depression

Some people with bipolar disorder may experience extreme negative thoughts, such as paranoia . Symptoms are common in psychotic depression. Psychotic symptoms can also be present. The treatment for psychotic depression is usually medical.

❖ Mixed depression

If you experience a severe episode of depression and have symptoms typical of hypomania or manic episodes, you may be experiencing mixed depression.

HOW STRONG IS YOUR DEPRESSION?

Bipolar disorder can cause a depression that is mild or severe. It may be helpful to create a list of the symptoms you experience during a bout of depression or mixed depression.This can help identify your typical warning or early symptoms which means that you can implement strategies for managing your depres- sion before it gets too severe. Recognizing symptoms that can persist between episodes allows you to reduce or eliminate them.

A full major depressive episode is a group of five or more persistent symptoms that last at least two weeks. One of these symptoms could be depressed mood, loss of enjoyment, or depressed mood. Episodes can range in severity depending on how intense they are.

How severe the symptoms of depression can be and how they impact your daily life, relationships, and safety. Some people experience a gradual progression from feeling tired and drained to feeling more energetic and having severe negative thoughts. There are also variations in the frequency and length of depressive episodes.

Although medical treatment is the best option for major depressive episodes, researchers have found that psychotherapy and medication can more effectively reduce depressive relapses in bipolar disorder. The appropriate support of others can also help prevent depressive episodes and reduce their severity

Mild depression that lasts for a few years

People living with bipolar disorder may experience an ongoing, milder form of depression lasting at least three years. This is called Dysthymic disorder. Sometimes people don't realize they have mild depression. This may cause them to feel depressed and may not be able to cope with the treatment.

A few symptoms between episodes

Some people are still left with a few symptoms of depression, which can hang around for months like an uninvited guest even when the full depressive episode is over. These lingering symptoms are sometimes referred to as residual or subsyndromal symptoms. They may not be too annoying and can clear up reasoning fast. But other times, residue symptoms can disrupt everyday life and require treatment in their own right. Residual symptoms may make it is harder to cope and increasing your risk of relapse.

Early symptoms and warning signs

Depression can strike people with bipolar disorder suddenly. Some people notice signs and symptoms early in the development of depression. These symptoms are often called 'prodromes' because they can precede the entire episode and act as a warning sign. Prodromes are difficult to recognize, but knowing the subtle changes in your mood, thoughts, and behavior that could indicate depression is a good way to get help and reduce the chance of relapse.

KEY POINTS

- Bipolar disorder is characterized by depression in the majority of people.

Depression does not define you.

- Depression is more severe, persistent, and disruptive than the temporary lows that everyone experiences due to everyday ups or downs.

- Although depression can sometimes feel overwhelming and devastating, it is treatable.

- People may have different combinations of depressive symptoms. Sometimes, depressive symptoms can be combined with hypomania or mania.

There may be different degrees of depression. A list of symptoms you experience in depression episodes can help you identify milder symptoms and warning signs.

- Some people experience depressive symptoms in between episodes. They are finding ways to manage these might make a difference in your daily life.

- It can be difficult to recognize the early signs and symptoms of depression, but it is possible to recover more quickly if you catch them earlier.

MANIA AND HYPOMANIA

Every person with bipolar disorder experiences hypomania at one time. Your experience may differ from that of someone with the same illness because you might have different levels of severity or various combinations of symptoms. Hypomania is a milder type of manic depression. These moods can be either elevated or "high" and can include extreme exuberance, more active feelings, and a higher level of confidence. Hypomania and mania symptoms can vary depending on the severity of your symptoms.

Hypomania and mania, like depression, can have various severity levels and clusters of symptoms. This information can help you catch the signs early to prevent relapse.

A case of hypomania or mania

A case of hypomania or mania is an episode that causes an irritable, expansive, or elevated mood. It can also include a cluster of at most three symptoms (four if you are irritable). These symptoms include increased activity, risk-taking, pleasure-seeking, and speeding up thoughts and speech.

Mania

Manic people will do certain things when they are feeling maniacal, like engage in risky activities.

Neglecting people, engaging in sexual activity, or investing in financial products, could have grave consequences. Some people may experience psychotic symptoms such as hallucinations, delusions, and changes in thinking when mania is very severe. Some people do not experience psychosis but may experience some symptoms such as delusions or hallucinations and marked differences in their thinking.

Hypomania

Hypomania and mania are two different things.

Hypomania is when people are not affected by the same level of disruption as full manic episodes. Those people may need hospitalization or experience psychotic symptoms. People not suffering from full mania may feel more creative, more able to work at home and socialize, and more able to achieve their goals when they are less depressed.

When you are in an early or mild mania, or when you tare hypomanic, the world truly is your oyster. The energy feeding in opens your mind a bit more and moves you a little faster. It lets you reach further for what was previously just beyond your reach.

The darker side

Hypomania can be a frustrating experience.

This can lead to increased irritability, hypersensitivity, and a feeling of being restless. This can lead to a loss of important relationships. Many people also experience "dysphoric mania," a combination of some manic and some depression symptoms. This can lead to a more severe condition. Classic mania can cause you to feel euphoric and overconfident or excessively optimistic. A mixed trend can cause manic symptoms like increased energy, decreased sleep, racing thoughts, speech, and anxiety. Your mood may also be unstable (changeable). This can be very distressing, and you are at greater risk of self-harm. It is important to seek immediate treatment.

Mixed mania is a diagnosis that DSM-IV requires both manic and depressive episodes to be present. However, some research suggests that as little as two or three of these depressive symptoms--depressed mood , depressed thoughts, guilt, fatigue, or anxiety--may be enough for diagnosis.

How to treat episodes

The best treatment for manic and hypomanic symptoms episodes are medical treatment. The effectiveness of mood-stabilizing medications in reducing the risk of future manic episodes has been impressive. This is due to the biological reasons for this disorder.

A few symptoms

Bipolar I and II disorders can sometimes cause mild symptoms. It is easy to recognize warning signs or prodromes for hypomania or mania. This will allow you to prevent a relapse or minimize its consequences.

WHAT HAPPENS IF YOU ARE HYPOMANIC or MANIC?

Hypomanic or manic symptoms can cause various changes in your behavior, thoughts, and feelings.

Activity changes.

Be aware of any changes in your behavior. They are the easiest to make.

Do more than you usually do

This activity increase may seem to be organized and produced. Intense, especially in the beginning, but then becomes more frenetic.

Agitation and restlessness

It is possible to become disoriented and wander from one task or another.

You feel so excited that you find it difficult to remain still and achieve your goals.

You need to sleep less.

You might feel like you have lots of energy and aren't sleeping as much as normal.

Be more conversational

As a result, your speech might become faster, louder, and more compressed.

It is more difficult for people to interrupt or have their say.

Set more goals

Your attention may be directed to other areas. To pursue your goals, you may have to sacrifice your normal activity, sleep schedule, and other important responsibilities. As you get sicker, your dreams can grow more complicated and unattainable.

Don't forget to eat

Sometimes, basic physical needs like eating can feel trivial. When people become manic, they seem to be able to survive on very little food.

You take more chances and be more impulsive. Initial signs of a change may be subtle.

Some people are less careful at work, less cautious driving, more open to sharing their opinions with others, and more sexually provocative in how they dress and spend money.

These subtle changes indicate the onset of more dangerous risky behaviors such as reckless driving and entering into suspect business deals.

You can change the way that you relate to others.

Hypomaniacs often appear to have the ability to see what is going on.

They have the right words to say and can be a very engaging company. However, they can become impatient, snappy, defensive, and irritable when challenged or thwarted. Your mania can increase, and you may become more intrusive, socially inappropriate, impatient, and argumentative when contradicted or frustrated.

Aggressiveness and irritability

Dysphoric mania sufferers may become very irritable.

Sometimes, the symptoms can be aggressive or be bizarre in behavior.

Feeling depressed or manic.

Hypo-manic or manic symptoms can cause noticeable changes in your moods, leading to more intense feelings.

Emotional mood elevation or euphoria

It is possible to feel better than you used to, up to a point.

It is not related or disproportional to what is happening in your life then.

You have a lot of energy

It may seem as though you can go on for hours without stopping.

Enhanced senses

Hypomania and Mania seem to increase colors and natural beauty.

All sounds, smells, and tastes are magnified.

Spirituality or religion?

Many people report experiencing mystical feelings of oneness with God or nature.

Some people experience an increase in their desire for sex.

Self-confidence and self-importance are increased.

Some people feel more in control of their power and are more capable.

To achieve success, they may believe their actions, personalities, and words have some unique significance. People may feel like they are bulletproof when they're manic. These moods can cause self-confidence that is obvious to others. People in hypomanic and manic states are extremely convincing to the outsiders. Their unusual behavior, lack of logic, and risky behavior alert those around them to their condition. This creates concern and raises concerns.

More social

Some people have a greater need to connect with others.

Sensitivity increases. Some people are sensitive to criticism and can be defensive.

Irritability

Feeling angry or irritable in general or with particular people? It is common to meet people who cannot keep up with you or condemn your risky endeavors. People can suddenly switch from extreme euphoria and extreme irritability. This makes it hard for you and others to keep up with your pace and may even cause you to become angry.

Impulsiveness and impatience

Sometimes it can be hard to wait, postpone or delay being satisfied. You will want it even if it's risky or potentially dangerous.

Feeling up, but not down

While you may have some of the typical symptoms of manic or hypomanic, you might feel sad, tired, or anxious.

Spin-out of control

Sometimes people feel like they're losing control because of their surroundings.

Psychotic symptoms or impulsivity can be very distressing for people who love them.

Hypomanic and manic thinking

Common changes in how you see yourself, others, the future, and your thinking are common.

Consider yourself to be powerful

You might see yourself as strong and capable of doing great things. You may be able to do great things.

Hypomania can be a normal state of mind. Having more confidence in yourself may even help. Your view of yourself can become more unrealistic and grandiose as you get sicker. Sometimes people make huge and risky commitments that they regret later.

Rose-colored glasses: Seeing the world through rose-colored glasses.They can lose sight of the risks and end up doing things that could have devastating effects on their lives.

Extreme views of others

Hypomanic or manic behavior can lead to judgments of others.

You may be very positive about other people's good qualities and attractiveness or hypercritical.

Negative thinking is more common

Mixed mania can confuse your view.

More in common with depression is pessimism, negative thinking about others, and low self-esteem.

Racing thoughts

Though thoughts can seem quicker when you're mildly hypomanic, your thinking may slow down. As you get sicker, they run away with your brain.

Unorganized thinking

Your attention can wander from one point to another, even though it is clear and concise. This can lead to a maniacal state where you cannot focus on one thing or remember the details.

Another is based only on the most tenuous connections. If you're talking about a shopping trip, your thoughts might suddenly shift to the Apollo mission to the moon. These thoughts, expressed in speech, are not understood by the observer. People with bipolar disorder have been able to create great art and ideas by seeing unusual connections between objects. But, some people with bipolar disorder can have trouble seeing the links and be unable to see clearly.

When they are manic, people have many more ideas and plans. This can lead to productive action. However, their ideas may become more absurd and unrealistic as mania worsens. You can lose focus by trying to achieve multiple goals, disrupting sleep and your normal routines.

Increase your belief in your ideas and opinions

These ideas are often viewed as more urgent, and there is an increased urgency to act.

Bizarre thinking

People can develop delusions, which are fixed beliefs that have no foundation.

Reality about their abilities and authority, or paranoid delusions (in more dysphoric mania) about the people against them. When they believe they are receiving messages, they can experience auditory or visual hallucinations.

People with bipolar disorder might miss hypomania or even 'euphoric mania.' People may be lured by the promise of success to prolong their hypomania and mania rather than taking steps to address them. People may even try to trigger mania by stopping a treatment or using stimulants. They often suffer from the negative effects of euphoric sensation. Another problem with these elevated moods is their inability to stay positive. Many people fall into depression and mixed mania. Most people who experience hypomania do not have focus. It is their depression that causes them to seek treatment.

Mania is not your fault. Manic episodes can lead to other mental illnesses. Manic episodes can cause guilt and shame, leading to additional stress and depression..

KEY POINTS

- Hypomania is a common symptom of bipolar disorder.

Mania and manic episodes at one point in time, with symptoms that can vary in severity and combination.

- Understanding your hypomania and mania patterns can help reduce the effects of bipolar disorder.

- You can monitor your condition and take steps to reduce or prevent future episodes by listing common symptoms you may experience during a manic or hypomanic episode.

- Disturbing or disruptive behavior indicates illness and is not your fault.

- Hypomania and mania can be a temporary state of pleasure and productivity for some. However, this feeling is often short-lived and quickly transforms into depression and mixed conditions.

- Even though mania can be a pleasant experience, it can devastate your relationships, financial security, and occupations.

- Effective treatment includes medication, psychotherapy, and personal strategies.

BIPOLAR DISORDER ADAPTING

Bipolar disorder is not just about the symptoms. It also affects how you live your daily life. Bipolar disorder is an individual experience that many people struggle to accept. This chapter will discuss the different ways people adapt to bipolar disorder. These can include denying you have it or blaming everything on it. Or they are actively seeking out the high moods. There is sometimes no middle ground. This involves accepting the disorder and flexibility between a focus and a life-focused approach depending on your symptoms. People may switch between these approaches at different times in their lives. Many people find a way to manage their illness to live a full and healthy life.

DENIAL AFTER FIRST DIAGNOSED

Think about what it was like to be diagnosed with bipolar disorder. Sometimes, there's some relief after being diagnosed with bipolar disorder.

As when I was diagnosed, it can cause you to think deeply about your identity and how it will impact your future. Stigma and misconceptions about the condition may have shaped your perception of bipolar disorder. Some respond with defiance to the diagnosis and attribute their symptoms externally to diet, work stress, exhaustion, conflicts, or their personality.

There are milder forms as well. 'Under-identification' may involve some acknowledgment of the disorder but without real acceptance or ownership. This can be a denial that means you are aware of your bipolar disorder but want to forget it. It also could mean not following through with treatment and lifestyle changes. This is also common for other illnesses. People with heart problems, for example, may not be able to accept their diagnosis, but they will continue to think about it. Acceptance is essential to managing your illness. However, this can be difficult. It is easier to accept the condition when you have had more than one episode.

How to deal with difficult emotions

People sometimes use denial to protect themselves from the most difficult emotions, such as anger and shame. These emotions may return from time to again as you learn ways to live with your illness.

People living with bipolar disorder have said that they experience grief when they grieve for the person they used to be and the changes and losses they've experienced. You are not the only one who has experienced sadness at such loss and change. I know that I did.

Management of bipolar disorder requires you to find new ways to see yourself. This includes recognizing your strengths and talents and taking into consideration your vulnerability. You may also need to accept the loss and find new meaning and fulfillment.

Shame and humiliation

Learning about their diagnosis can cause shame and humiliation for some people.

This feeling may occur after you have recovered from an episode where you did something that was not aligned with your standards or who you are. Sometimes it can be helpful to remember that although the bipolar disorder may be something you have, it is not your identity (Miklowitz 2002:56).

It is possible to blame yourself for the drop in your status and inability to meet certain standards and expectations.

Bipolar disorder can cause problems with your attention, memory, and daily functioning. Some people feel depressed and hopeless when they cannot live up to their set standards. You may find it more difficult to accomplish your goals during times of illness. The stress and pressure of pursuing unrealistic goals can make you more susceptible to relapse. People with bipolar disorder may set high standards and push for unrealistic goals. You may need to assess your strengths, talents, and interests to recover your self-esteem. Then, you will need to find other manageable, meaningful goals that consider your illness's limitations.

Shameful and humiliating stigmatizations about illness and its consequences can lead to shame and humiliation. If you are close to the stigma, it can be difficult to see past it. You and your loved ones can deal with this stigmatized illness through denial. Denial can also hinder or stop effective treatment.

Even those living with bipolar disorder for many years can still find it stigmatizing. It is important to recognize the stigma and not be influenced by it. People who have lived with bipolar disorder report that they can accept their condition and feel positive about themselves, assert their rights, and live a fulfilling life.

Guilt

Bipolar disorder can make some people feel guilty.

They have brought it on themselves. Although people can control bipolar disorder by trying their best, it is still a partly genetic illness. Bipolar disorder is not your fault.

Even if it means you must face the consequences, it can be crucial to be able to see your illness at work again when you are feeling well.

Anger

It is normal to ask why you have chronic diseases like other chronic conditions?

This? Why? Sometimes you may feel angry about the illness, the losses, and limitations. Family members might feel the brunt. Sometimes, it is helpful to find constructive ways to express anger, such as writing or painting. When your illness is treated effectively, anger can often subside, and you feel more confident and able to enjoy your life again. It is normal to feel frustrated or angry when faced with something unfair.

Fear

What bipolar disorder is and what it can mean for you and your future can lead to fear, anxiety, and attempts to ignore the diagnosis, or it can cause constant worry and efforts for relapse prevention. This fear can be reduced by learning more about bipolar disorder and effective ways to manage your illness and live a full life.

It can be confusing to discover that you have bipolar disorder. Talk to a trusted clinician to learn more about the different types of bipolar disorder, treatment options, and how to manage your symptoms.

DENIAL BEFORE MANY EPISODES

Bipolar disorder does not have to be an one-size-fits-all situation. Denial can still be helpful even after years of struggle with bipolar disorder. It may help you avoid frustrations due to your illness, some ongoing depressive symptoms, and the trauma or disappointment of a relapse. Sometimes, even after several episodes, denial can be a way to protect yourself from the stigmatizing effects of your illness.

Bipolar moods can cause people to question their diagnosis. Sometimes depression can seem very real to life, leading people to believe they aren't ill. However, people who become manic are more likely to reject the illness and need treatment.

BIPOLAR DISORDER ADAPTION

No matter how many episodes someone has experienced, it doesn't matter how many. Sometimes these practical problems require you to make plans with your doctor or other professionals about how you will manage them if they occur.

People who have been well for a while may be tempted to downplay or question the diagnosis and need for treatment. People who have had bipolar disorder for many years may need to check whether it is a recurring illness or if they were properly diagnosed. If so, they might stop taking their medication. This testing is normal, but it can pose a real risk to the patient.

BECOMING ILL

Some people who accept a diagnosis of bipolar disorder are more accepting than others and view themselves as the disorder. This approach has a positive side. It allows you to acknowledge your illness and can be helpful when you're experiencing symptoms. If you have been through many episodes, rapid cycling, or are currently sick, it is easy to see yourself as the illness. You may find it difficult to enjoy life and rebuild your health.

Over-acceptance of or 'over-identification' with your illness can mean that everything that happens, even when you are well, is explained by bipolar disorder (Miklowitz, 2002). If you feel well and argue with someone rudely, your reactions may be attributed to your illness.

People with bipolar disorder can have difficulty adapting to changes in their lifestyles and necessary restrictions. However, they may also place unnecessary and excessive limitations on their lives and themselves. If they are anxious about relapsing, this may be a sign that they are experiencing a relapse.

Focusing on living well within the limitations of illness can make it difficult to cope with it. It can also lead to feeling unnecessarily depressed and hopeless. It isn't always easy to distinguish between the necessary and the unnecessary limits. In other words, finding the right balance between managing your illness and enriching it can be difficult.

SEARCHING FOR SYMPTOMS

Some people seek out stimulants and other ways to become hypomanic or manic. This can be costly. Living with uncontrolled mania, a mixed state, or the dark side of depression and the consequences on your life and those around you is hard.

You can take control of your symptoms so you can enjoy creativity, joy, and success without worrying about the negative consequences of untreated illnesses.

CAUSES AND TRIGGERS

Many people with bipolar disorder have questions about why they experience this illness. Bipolar disorder: What is the cause? Many people will answer "family arguments" or "work stress," but stress is not the cause. Like any other illness or condition, the underlying cause is biological. You can manage the course of your bipolar disorder by using constructive strategies.

STRESS VULNERABILITY MODEL

Biological vulnerability is a person's inability to recognize the symptoms of a specific illness. This vulnerability can still be present even if you don't feel the symptoms.

Some people may be predisposed to certain illnesses such as diabetes, hypertension, asthma, and elevated chlosterol. Bipolar disorder is more complicated than it seems. We know more about the causes of relapses and how they affect the course of the illness. However, we do know that childhood abuse is a risk factor for bipolar disorder.

Stress is often grouped with factors that can trigger the biological vulnerability. Stress refers to any pressure or expectation placed on us by our environment (for instance, family conflict) and ourselves (for example, high expectations). While a certain amount of stress can motivate someone's life, too much stress can cause them to feel overwhelmed and affect their health. Some stressors can trigger biological vulnerabilities that are not yet present and cause symptoms.

People not predisposed to bipolar disorder do not experience the same effects from these stressors. The following stressors can trigger bipolar episodes:

- Major stressful events or the accumulation of daily problems

- Overstimulation

- Activity or sleep disruptions

- Interpersonal conflict

- Drugs and alcohol

- Physical illness

Although a stressor does not automatically mean it will trigger bipolar episodes, it can increase your risk if it is a particularly stressful situation. You will be more sensitive if you have already been diagnosed with bipolar disorder. Knowing your triggers for illness can help you take steps to reduce their impact on your mood.

Sometimes, episodes of illness can occur without any triggers. You may be more sensitive to stress and have more relapses. This means that it takes less stress for you to get off the ground. Many people notice that mood swings are more common in those with more episodes than others, even if there isn't a major stressor.

The stress vulnerability model assumes that biological factors like genetics, such as the presence of bipolar disorder in your family, are strong. You might only need a mild stressor (such as a few late night hours) to trigger the illness. Individual stress thresholds are different for each person. Bipolar disorder can affect other people in different ways. Identifying the stressors that trigger your symptoms and finding ways to decrease their influence on your life is possible.

Your role is important because, despite your biological vulnerability and stressors and the fact that you can affect whether or not you relapse, how you manage and cope with your illness will impact whether you retreat. Hypomania can be prevented by not drinking too much alcohol. Recognizing triggers can help you avoid relapse by focusing your attention on them. Bipolar disorder can be reduced by managing your triggers and having psychotherapy.

Bipolar disorder can be caused by genetic and brain changes, such as changes in brain structure, chemicals, and functions. It also includes hormonal and immune changes.

Genetics

Bipolar disorder is a common disorder that runs in families but is not a completely genetic condition. Bipolar disorder is seven to twenty times more common in children born to parents with bipolar disorder than in those with it. However, this does not necessarily prove that bipolar disorder is genetic.

Identical twins share all genes. Twin studies compare similar twins with non-identical ones who share approximately half their genes, like brothers and sisters. The chances of bipolar disorder in one twin are 60-80%. The risk of developing bipolar disorder in siblings and non-identical twins is about 20%. All identical twins could develop the disease if it was 100% genetic. Genetics can be a contributing factor, but other factors are also important.

Bipolar disorder is thought to involve multiple genes rather than one gene. This makes it more difficult to pass it on. Bipolar disorder can be found in just 10% of children who have had a parent with the disease.

People with bipolar disorder often worry that they will pass the disease on to their children. However, this is not always possible. If you have children, you'll be able to educate them about bipolar disorder and the treatment options. Bipolar disorder can now be diagnosed early and treated effectively. This will help eliminate much of the suffering caused by late diagnosis or misdiagnosis.

A few factors can complicate bipolar disorder genetic studies. People with bipolar disorder often have their relatives suffer from major (or unipolar) depression. Bipolar disorder can also be caused by schizophrenia and depression.

Both genetic and environmental factors are important. People with bipolar disorder have a higher likelihood of their family members using drugs and alcohol. While some people with a family history of bipolar disorder may develop a psychiatric condition, others do not. Bipolar disorder is a result of a combination of genes and environmental stressors.

The idea that genetic vulnerability and environmental triggers interact is similar to how we understand many other medical conditions. If you are at high risk for developing heart disease due to high cholesterol, high blood pressure or poor diet, stress, and lack of physical activity can all increase your risk. This is where medication can be used to lower cholesterol and blood pressure. You also need to change your lifestyle, such as quitting smoking, getting more exercise, changing your diet, or reducing stress. This is similar to managing bipolar disorder. We use mood stabilizers to treat the underlying condition. Lifestyle changes are made to minimize the chance of relapse.

Brain changes

Bipolar disorder is characterized by brain differences that have given rise to valuable insights into the biological causes.

Brain chemicals

Chemical imbalances are a major cause of the bipolar disorder. These imbalances are treated with medication.

Neurotransmitters or chemical signals sent by nerve cells to each other by the brain, are chemical signals. They can be thought of as chemical emails. To communicate, one cell can send many neurotransmitters to another. These neurotransmitters include serotonin and noradrenaline, as well as dopamine, and gamma-aminobutyric acids (GABA).

Bipolar disorder patients may have their neurotransmitters altered in quantity or how they function. The limbic system is the brain area that regulates mood. Neurotransmitters play a role in their regulation.

Dopamine is a key component of drive, reward, and motivation. These moods are elevated in mania and decreased in depression. The fact that abuse of drugs such as amphetamines can trigger bipolar episodes suggests the role of dopamine in the development of the bipolar disorder.

Neurotransmitters attach to nerve cells through receptors that behave like sockets and plugs. After the neurotransmitters are connected to the nerve cells, second messengers (or chemicals) can be activated. Many second messengers are available, including G proteins, protein-kinase C, and calcium. People with bipolar disorder have these messenger systems altered. Mood stabilizers like lithium regulate second messengers.

Nerve growth factors

Neurotrophic factors are nerve growth factors or neurotrophic factors produced by the brain.

These are essential for the survival and function of specific nerve cells in the brain. Bipolar disorder may be caused by decreased survival-promoting and nerve cell growth factors in certain brain regions. Mood stabilizers increase nerve growth factors and may prevent some brain changes observed in people with bipolar disorder. A timely, consistent, and appropriate treatment can prevent brain changes and improve everyday functioning.

Sleep and clocks

Bipolar people are likely to have an extremely sensitive body clock that reacts rapidly and violently to signal changes.

Everybody has an internal clock that sets the body's cycles. This includes the sleep/wake cycle that determines when you fall asleep and when you wake up. The body clock regulates hormones and chemicals that affect vital biological functions such as blood pressure, temperature, and hormone secretion. A suprachiasmatic nuclear nucleus is a small group of nerves in the hypothalamus, the middle of your brain. The setting of an individual's body clock may be affected by genetics. Bipolar disorder patients may experience changes in their clock speed. Lithium may also affect the genes that regulate this clock.

Regular activities, regular sleep patterns, and social stimulation are all factors that can help you set your body clock. Melatonin, released when light is present, is affected by the time you go to bed and wake up and helps regulate your sleep/wake cycles. People living with bipolar disorder are especially sensitive to changes in their daily rhythms, such as sleep and activity patterns. You may experience disruptions in your daily rhythms due to jet lag, shift work, major life events like a death or a move, or even minor changes such as a change in working hours. A single night of sleeplessness can cause mania in sensitive individuals. Hypomania and mania can be caused by sleep loss. This can also lead to a symptom or illness that increases the severity of the condition. People with mood disorders may experience more episodes of depression if there is less light in the autumn and winter. This vulnerability affects 20-30% of bipolar disorder patients.

Immune changes

The body's defense against infection is called the immune system. To fight infection, it uses both immune cells as well as chemicals. There are people with bipolar disorder and ordinary depression show subtle immune changes.

Hormones

Cortisol, a hormone secreted by adrenal glands during stressful times, can be found in the blood. People with bipolar disorder may have excess cortisol. Cortisol can affect the brain and nerve cells. Research is underway to develop new medications that target bipolar disorder and cortisol.

KEY POINTS

- Genetic predisposition is one of the biological causes of bipolar disorder.

- Changes to the brain (including brain structures and activity in certain brain regions), changes in the regulation of the body clock, and hormonal and immune changes in your body.

- An individual may experience an episode of illness if they have multiple triggers, and biology is not the only thing that can cause it.

- You can change the course of your illness by using constructive coping skills, such as psychotherapy and medication combined with psychotherapy, managing your warning signs and triggers, and living a healthy lifestyle.

- Negative coping strategies like alcohol and drugs can also worsen your illness.

MANAGING WARNING SYMPTOMS OF HYPOMANIA or MANIA

There are ways to avoid relapse if you have hypomania or mania symptoms. People who use constructive strategies to deal with their warning signs, such as talking to their doctor, resting, and doing some calming, have fewer relapses. They are more successful in their relationships and work lives than those who resort to unhelpful ways of coping.

You can plan to prevent or reduce hypomanic and manic relapse by identifying key warning signs and providing basic instructions on what to do. This will allow you to respond quickly, constructively, and early. This chapter focuses on consulting your doctor and strategies to reduce overactivity and restore sleep. It also addresses early thinking changes that can be used to detect early signs and prevent relapse. We will be discussing ways to avoid some of the unpleasant consequences of mania.

Keep these things in your mind

If you want to avoid an episode, timing is crucial. Many people don't know when they have reached the top of the roller-coaster. They may lose sight of the fact that they're ill as they become hypomanic and manic. This can make it difficult for them to take medication or use helpful strategies to manage their symptoms. It is important to recognize warning signs early and respond promptly.

You can choose how you respond to your illness even though you are separate from it accepting that your hypomanic mood can temporarily affect your thoughts and feelings. You don't have to act on these feelings. You have the opportunity to implement your relapse prevention strategies. You and your loved ones can put your illness in perspective. This will help reduce guilt, shame, and disruption in your life.

Many people recognize that they can cycle from hypomania to mania to depression. They take immediate action to decrease their hypomania and mania, so they don't get depressed. Others are determined to act.

Avoid or reduce the effects of mania to avoid the negative consequences and disruption it can cause. People are encouraged to know that there are effective ways to prevent and minimize relapse.

EARLY TREATMENT

If you recognize signs of bipolar disorder and call your doctor to seek help, you can stop a manic episode from developing by taking the prescribed medication. It is important to keep in touch with your doctor regularly and have regular follow-ups. If things get more serious, your doctor can assess your mood and arrange hospitalization.

Your doctor might arrange for you to take additional medication when you feel you have episodes. Keep an eye on your mood and tell your doctor if it changes. If things aren't improving, you might need to ask your doctor to see you sooner than the next appointment. You can reduce your chances of hospital admission by catching manic symptoms early. Some people have other professionals involved in their care, such as a psychologist, a case manager, or a psychiatrist. It may be beneficial to reach out to them to help you develop strategies to avoid relapse.

Slow down

Research has shown that bipolar disorder can cause disruptions in your daily activities, social stimulation, and sleep patterns. This can disrupt your body's circadian rhythms and lead to hypomania and mania. Hypomania is when you feel depressed or irritable.

You may feel like you've suddenly jumped into the fast lane with many ideas. Your activity level increases and you fall asleep less. This disruption can lead to a deeper episode of illness or spin.

Put the brakes on

People with bipolar disorder recommend several strategies to decrease stimulation, restore routines and improve sleep patterns.

Get more sleep

Hypomania and Mania can be triggered by too little sleep.

Many people find that controlling their sleep helps them to feel more stable. Experts recommend that you increase your sleep time to at least 10 hours with the temporary help of medication prescribed by your physician. You could try this for several days to prevent hypomania and mania as an emergency plan.

Reduce overstimulation

Take into account what you find too stimulating. Consider, if you are experiencing warning signs, avoid crowds, social situations, and other arrangements that could cause irritability, aggression, or impulsive behavior.

Reducing caffeine

Reduce caffeine in coffee, teas, chocolate, and energy drinks, even multivitamins and any other stimulants.

Reduce aggravation

Check to see if things are temporarily aggravating around you like loud TV, music, clutter, and children's toys. Reduced stimulation can be made a shared effort by inviting the help of your family.

Choose calming activities

You may be struggling with a lot of energy and difficulty.

Sitting still is better than sitting down. Choose the least stimulating activity. If you don't feel like running 10 km but know that you'll feel more energetic afterward, you can choose to walk around the block or take a friend for a ride. Don't try to exhaust yourself with more activity and exercise. This will only make you more stimulated and cause you to be more hypomanic.

Reduce the number of activities

Plan fewer activities per week to reduce overactivity.

You should act as if you have the flu. This means lots of rest, TV, a few outings, and tranquility. Avoid scheduling things for the evening, particularly if they are stimulating, as these may keep you awake. You can prepare calming activities like sitting in the garden, taking an easy bath, relaxing in dim lighting, or doing relaxation exercises. You can monitor your mood by observing how your activities affect your mood. You can restore your normal routine and sleep habits once your mood stabilizes. However, you should include calming activities to help you recover.

Prioritizing goals and tasks

There may be many tasks and goals you wish to accomplish.

Limit your activities, not increase them. This will help you achieve your goals. Here are some ways to cut down.

- Do not delay or eliminate goals that aren't essential. Sometimes it is helpful to get the assistance of others.

Trust others to help you prioritize them. You should list all the goals or tasks you are considering. Ask yourself the following question: "If I had to, can I do this without a specific goal? Or can I postpone it?" Extend your timeframes to turn some of your current goals into long-term ones. This will allow you to lower your activity level. You can cross the task off your list if it is not necessary. If it can be postponed, put a 'P' next. To give yourself the freedom to slow down and delegate tasks. Write 'D' next to the job if you can trust it or part of it to someone else. Identity high, medium, and low priorities from the remaining tasks and goals. Prioritize goals that lead to success over all else.

- To eliminate goals, you can assess them individually to determine if they are realistic and if you have considered the potential dangers and negative consequences.

- You can schedule forced breaks to allow yourself quiet time. Also, you should stick to regular meals, bedtimes, and waking times, regardless of your goals.

PSYCHOTHERAPY

Psychotherapy is a treatment that uses strategies and techniques to improve a person's well-being and life. Sometimes called "talk therapy," psychotherapy can be described as a passive process that overlooks the work involved in working through a problem.

Although psychotherapy cannot replace medication or cure bipolar disorder, it can help you make positive changes. The specifics of what is involved vary depending on the type of psychotherapy used and the individual's needs. Bipolar disorder can be managed with a few types of therapy.

A therapist may be able to help you:

- Learn more about bipolar disorder and how to treat it

- Have more control over your illness if you can identify and manage the triggers and early warning signs

- Develop a plan to prevent relapse

- Reduce symptoms of anxiety and depression

- Talk through your problems to reduce stress

- Get back on your feet following an episode of illness.

- Develop a healthy lifestyle

- Learn to accept your bipolar disorder and find ways to live a fulfilled life.

You might have experienced a disruptive episode in your life that has caused problems at work or in relationships. This may be why you want to learn more about the disorder and how it affects your life. You might have specific concerns or worries about issues like whether to tell your coworkers or if you should disclose the condition to your partner.

DIFFERENT TYPES THERAPY

In addition to bipolar disorder medication, there are many other types of therapy. Psychotherapy has two goals: to keep you well, prevent or minimize relapses and their consequences, and improve your quality of life. Although each approach to this goal is different, they all emphasize collaboration between your therapist and yourself. They highlight information about bipolar disorder, the importance of knowing your triggers and moods, and how to help you manage them.

Psychoeducation

Psychoeducational approaches emphasize information about bipolar disorder, its treatment, and how to treat it. Psychoeducation is an important aspect of most psychotherapy for bipolar disorder. It highlights key elements such as:

- Types of bipolar disorder and their course
- Stress and its triggers, early detection of warning signs, and early recognition
- Medication

- Positive ways to cope include a healthy lifestyle and stress management.

Cognitive and cognitive-behavioral therapy Cognitive therapy (CT) and cognitive-behavioral treatment (CBT) both focus on the relationship between thoughts (cognitions), behavior (the actions you take), and how you feel. This approach focuses on changing certain thought patterns and beliefs that can lead to negative changes in behaviors and worsening of your mood.

❖ Family-focused therapy

Family-focused therapy is an inclusive approach to bipolar disorder, including the individual with the disease and their family members. It aims to improve interaction and support among family members and resolve conflict within the family. To prevent relapse, the family works together.

Psychoeducation, problem-solving, and communication skills are the three main components of this form of therapy. This can be done by having family discussions.

- Family members can learn more about the disorder, its biology, stressors, and coping strategies through the psychoeducation sessions.

- The communication sessions promote positive feedback and counter dysfunctional communication styles. This is a sign that the family is struggling to deal with the disorder.

Family members can play active listening and make positive requests.

- Problem-solving is a tool that this approach uses to help families deal with disagreements and difficulties. Families work together to identify and evaluate possible solutions and create a plan of action.

Family-focused therapy can also be used to address the problem of suicide. This approach recognizes that suicidal thoughts and feelings are part of the disease. Talking about your feelings with family members and creating a suicide prevention plan together can help you get control of these troubling thoughts and feelings.

❖ **Interpersonal therapy and social rhythm therapy**.

Interpersonal therapy and social rhythm therapy (IPSRT) is a variation of interpersonal therapy (IPT). IPSRT emphasizes the importance of interpersonal relationships in mental well-being. The IPSRT recognizes the importance of grief and loss in bipolar disorder treatment and provides clients with the opportunity to share their feelings and find unique solutions.

The second key element of IPSRT for bipolar disorder is the patterns of everyday life and our social rhythms. This approach emphasizes the possibility that a disruption in regular social rhythms could lead to an episode of illness. People with bipolar disorder need to maintain a stable mood by having traditional day-night rhythms (circadian). These patterns include the time we wake up and go to bed and our normal activities like going to work or meeting with friends every morning. Participants in this therapy are asked to track their sleep/wake cycle, daily activity patterns, and stimulation levels. This includes the number of people they meet with. They can regulate their daily routines, so their mood does not get disturbed.

❖ Beginning Therapy

The approach to therapy can be different depending on the individual. Other systems may work better for certain people. For example, a family-focused method would be suitable in situations with obvious family problems. It is not about the therapy but also the choice of the right therapist. Having a good working relationship and trust with your therapist is important.

Here are some tips for starting psychotherapy:

- Ask friends, family members, or other consumers to recommend a therapist.

- You can find a therapist near you by visiting the websites of psychological societies.

- It is important to verify that the person you plan to meet with is properly qualified, registered, and has experience working with people with bipolar disorder.

- It is possible to ask them about their perspective when working with clients.

- You may want to know the number of sessions you will require. It can be hard to estimate, but it is important that you and your therapist have a regular review period. This will allow you to evaluate the progress of your sessions. Sometimes, the financial cost can limit the number of sessions.

- Regular appointments are easier to remember and fit into your daily routine.

- Don't be afraid to talk about cost. It is important to check the price of your therapy and whether your insurance covers it.

- You must be able to relate to the therapy at this time. You may have multiple issues, in addition to bipolar disorder. You may not pay attention to therapy sessions that explore symptoms of illness if you are going through a divorce or are being evicted. These times may require that issues other than bipolar illness be addressed more frequently.

- Identifying the problems or goals you are trying to solve may be useful. This could include learning strategies to avoid relapse and dealing with problematic relationships. This will help you decide what you want out of psychotherapy. If you have other concerns, you can always come back at a later time.

❖ Mindfulness-based Cognitive Therapy

Mindfulness-based cognitive therapy is a type of meditation that teaches people to be aware of their feelings, thoughts, and sensations and to modify their automatic reactions to them. These techniques can help manage depressive thoughts or feelings in people who have had unipolar episodes. Researchers are currently investigating the applicability to bipolar disorder.

KEY POINTS

- There are many different approaches to psychology that can be helpful.

When combined with medication, bipolar illness can be managed. These include:

- Psychoeducation
- Cognitive and cognitive behavioral therapy
- Family-focused therapy
- Treatment for interpersonal and social rhythms
- Information about the disorder, medications, triggers, and strategies to minimize relapse.

While there are some key differences between particular therapeutic approaches, no one therapy method has been proven superior. To help you find the right therapist, you can consult your doctor or other people whose opinions are important to you. These tips will help you get started with psychotherapy.

SUPPORT AND ACTIVITY STRATEGIES IF YOU ARE DEPRESSED

It is possible to avoid or reduce the severity of depression by recognizing and responding to early signs or symptoms. You can manage your depression episodes by taking medication or a combination of medication and psychotherapy.

- Contact your doctor and support network

- Maintaining or restoring your activity level

- Exercise and other enriching activities

- Restoring your sleep habits

- Avoid being pessimistic or undermining your thinking and making important decisions.

Unhelpful strategies include "doing nothing," staying in bed, sleeping all night, and using alcohol or other drugs.

Many people with bipolar disorder have developed a personal strategy to deal with depression. If a system has worked for you for some time, we recommend you keep it. We will discuss various approaches to managing depression symptoms in this chapter and the following chapters. This chapter focuses on enlisting your support network and restoring sleep and activity. These ideas can be included in your plan to prevent a depressive relapse.

Keep these things in your mind

Here are some helpful tips to help you remember when you start to feel depressed.

- "You are not your depression." Your mood is not your only thing. Depression can feel real and overwhelming and be a permanent part of your identity. However, it is just a mood. Depression symptoms can be a sign of a more serious illness. You can break free from the symptoms and take control of your life. It is easier to recognize depression early.

- Depression is not your fault. "Depression does not result from a failure to accept responsibility, fear of dealing with reality, laziness or cowardice, or weakness".

- There are many ways to cope with depression symptoms. It is normal to feel anxious if you suspect you are experiencing a depressive episode. There are many effective strategies and treatments to decrease depression. Talking about your concerns with someone you trust is a good idea.

MOBILISING YOUR SUPPORT NETWORK

❖ Contacting your clinician(s)

If you feel depressed, it is a good idea for you to talk to your doctor. Regular visits with your doctor will help you monitor your depression and implement your suicide prevention plan. If your depression is severe or you are at risk of suicide, your doctor may arrange for hospitalization. You can also contact your caseworker or psychotherapist to get help with strategies.

❖ Choose close friends or relatives

It can be more difficult to feel depressed if you are not isolated. However, many people with bipolar disorder report feeling worse when they have contact with certain people. There may be a few people that have a positive impact on your mood. Good support can reduce the likelihood of a depressive episode and depressive relapses.

While it is possible to receive support from family and friends in the form of them helping you with specific tasks, it could also be about feeling their love and belief in your abilities.

Here are some ways they might be involved.

- Learning more about bipolar depression and what it is like to experience it.

- Listening to you without criticizing or judging or expecting you to snap it out.'

- Asking what they can do for you.

- Supporting your positive strategies and helping to reduce stress triggers.

- Monitoring your symptoms can help you stay on top of things.

- Helping with tasks that seem overwhelming, but encouraging your efforts to keep a basic routine and to increase activity gradually.

- Distracting yourself by doing things together.

- Not making too many demands and allowing you to have space but being there.

- Reassuring that there are things you can do to help.

- Helping you if the depression becomes worse

- Encouraging you to call your doctor or have them call on your behalf

- If necessary, accompanying you to the appointment or hospital.

- Helping you cancel or delegate commitments when your depression becomes serious, or you are hospitalized

- Helping you to use your suicide prevention plan.

- Making urgent decisions on your behalf. They must know that temporary measures that require them to act for you are necessary due to illness. These will not apply when you are fully recovered.

- Visiting your hospital regularly if you are ill to show they care

- Encouraging you to use your constructive strategies to help you get back on track slowly after a bout of depression. Don't expect too much.

RESTORING ACTIVITY

Do you know how it feels to have a good conversation with someone, watch a funny film, or achieve something?

You might be surprised at how different things are from what you have been doing. Activities enrich our lives and help us to be more motivated. It can feel like you are wasting your time and not doing what you love. Even mild depression symptoms can impact your motivation, activity, and enjoyment.

Do something pleasurable

It is believed that pleasure can increase the immune system.

By making even five minutes of enjoyment, amusement, joy, interest, or laughter, you will be less likely to believe that your negative feelings are permanent and irreversible.

Doing something you once enjoyed can provide you with a sense of satisfaction or achievement, but it may become a distraction if you don't find much enjoyment in them. As you get more involved with the activity, the pleasure may return. You might find it helpful to start with easy activities, such as putting on your favorite clothes or walking in the garden. Then, you can move on to activities that require planning and input from others, such as going to a movie together.

Organize social activity

Depression can be exacerbated by being too isolated.

Although it may be natural to feel isolated, socializing can be distracting and fun. You have the option to choose who you want to be with. It can be beneficial to set small goals to improve your social contacts. If you've been canceling plans, you might consider joining the group for a specific time. If you have difficulty talking to people, it is worth going along with another person to do an activity, such as watching a movie or listening to music.

Organize the load

Some people find it difficult to organize and plan things.

However, once you're done with it, it can be a great way to reduce stress, especially if your symptoms are depression-related or you're recovering from a depressive episode. If you have a decreased activity level or are experiencing a depressive episode, this could be a sign that your activity levels are declining.

Are you feeling overwhelmed or unable to get things done? It can help you prioritize the most important tasks, delegate any that you can and create a timetable or weekly schedule. Consider the most urgent charges first if there are many. It is a good idea to pick challenging but not too difficult activities to help you get more done once you have completed them. It can be helpful to set an activity time, so you don't procrastinate.

It is a good idea to break down overwhelming tasks into smaller steps. For example, choose which room needs to be cleaned first instead of cleaning the entire house and then divide it into stages. Let's say you have to clean the kitchen. Start with the dishes, then move on to the next task. For example, wipe the benches and then sweep the floor. Some people prefer to give some time to jobs they don't feel like doing. You might decide to clean for half an hour today and then spend ten more minutes cleaning tomorrow. Then again, you could do the same thing the next day. It might be easier to focus on your work for half an hour, take a break and then work another half hour.

Building a healthy structure and restoring your activity levels

Determining how many activities you can schedule on a given day may be difficult. How depressed do you feel? It is important to take small steps to overcome lethargy. Then, slowly return to your normal daily activities. You may feel stressed or overwhelmed if you try to keep up with all the tasks. This could lead to mania or hypomania. It is important to keep track of how your actions affect your mood. You can assess your mood before and afterward to determine what works. You can then decide if you want to do more, less, or different types of activities.

Awareness is key to doing things

It is important to consider what activities you should include in your daily activity plan when you are experiencing depression symptoms and how you perform these activities. Depression is characterized by being only half-present when you are engaged in a task. Instead of focusing on the task, your focus will be on your depression or worries.

HELPFUL THINKING STRATEGIES TO RELIEVE DEPRESSION

Everybody has bad days. Everyone thinks negatively from time to time. Some people tend to see the glass half-empty rather than half-full due to their temperament or mild depression symptoms that occur between illnesses. People often report that they find their thinking more negative when stressed. This type of thinking is not a fleeting negative thought in difficult situations. It can cause negative associations and memories about yourself, the world, and the future. Negative thinking can be a symptom of depression. A rise in extreme, persistent, or rigid negative thinking is a warning sign of imminent lows. Negative thinking can make you feel more discouraged and immobilized, making you feel less productive and depressed. It can be very helpful to discover ways to stop negative thinking from dragging you down. This chapter offers some useful strategies.

DIFFERENT INTERPRETATIONS

There are many ways to interpret a situation. Interpretations are thoughts or 'selftalk' that we have with ourselves about the situation. Cognitive behaviorists believe that ideas and interpretations of situations can influence how you feel and do things. You might say, "I'm an idiot; I can do nothing right," if a meeting at work went poorly. You might feel irritable, sad, or even angry at yourself. This can make it difficult to concentrate and lead to poor work habits. Your work may suffer as a result. This can lead to negative thoughts about your job and cause you to feel more stressed.

You might also interpret the situation in the following way: "The meeting didn't go as planned, and this was due to a variety of factors, including everyone's poor preparation. It might be possible to sell more of our product if we spend more time preparing."

By examining your thinking and identifying more helpful and balanced perspectives, you can reduce biases, pessimistic or undermining reflection.

UNHELPFUL THINKING STYLES

There are several ways that your thinking can temporarily become unhelpful and illogical. This is especially true if you experience depression or mixed emotions (Basco 2006). This kind of thinking can cause you to feel worse and make it harder for you to see the real issues.

These common thinking distortions can be a hindrance to a balanced view.

These include but not limited to:

- Jumping to negative conclusions

- Exaggerating the negative

- Extremes

- Extreme shoulds

- Mind reading

- Personalizing

- Fortune-telling

- Blaming

- Overestimating the goodness and beauty of the world

- Over-generalizing

- Catastrophizing

- Labelling

Jumping to negative conclusions

Jumping to negative conclusions is a tendency to make quick judgments and assume the worst without understanding the whole story or ignoring contradictory evidence. It can be useful to examine all evidence before you make any judgments. These are some common ways to jump to conclusions:

Exaggerating the negative

Stress can cause you to magnify or magnify the bad and negative things that happen and minimize or dismiss the positive aspects of yourself, others, and the future. This can lead to worse feelings and make it more difficult to move on. It is important to have a balanced view that also considers the positives. You might exaggerate the good.

Extremes

Thinking in all or nothing is a tendency not to see things in a positive light.

Extreme ways can be interpreted as very good, 'terrible,' or both. This ignores the middle ground. It is important to look at the gray areas and see the other side of the story. You may be able to see the strengths and weaknesses in someone you know.

'Extreme shoulds'

"Extreme shoulds" include any rules that you might set.

You can feel very depressed if you cannot relate to others or your life. There are no perfect people. We all make mistakes; sometimes, things don't go as planned, and situations can become complicated. One person might succeed or understand in one case but not in another. You and others may behave differently in different situations. Therefore, dictating what should be done is unrealistic. It is better to have flexible standards that account for human fallibility and situation complexity. While it is normal to feel frustrated or angry when your expectations are not met, it can be useful to step back and look at the 'extreme oughts' to determine if you can be more accepting of yourself, others, and the world. It can help to recognize and replace I 'should' and I 'must' with I 'prefer'. I 'have to' with an I 'would love' to reduce the pressure from high standards. "I would like to be a great cook, but I'm good at other things, so it's not a disaster if I'm not as good as I'd like to be."

Unrealistic goals can lead to disappointment, disrupting routines, sleep, and illness. You can replace unrealistic expectations with realistic ones based on your strengths, weaknesses, timeframes, resources, other needs, and health.

Mind-reading

Mind-reading is a way to jump to negative conclusions.

It is a belief that you can read someone's mind and predict their thoughts. You might be surprised at how different his opinion is from yours. It may help to find out what he thinks. You can also remind yourself that nobody is a mind-reader. You can't read the mind of someone else so, for instance, if they smile at you, it could be that they love you. Mind-reading can cause disappointment, embarrassment, and even the end of relationships. You can avoid such negative consequences by remembering that people act the way they do because of many factors and that you might be wrong about their thoughts or intentions. Consider the consequences of working on a mistaken interpretation.

Personalizing

Personalizing means taking things personally and leaping to the next level.

You may conclude that any negative comments or incidents you hear are about you. This is especially true if you feel depressed or irritable or suspicious. There may be many reasons people behave or respond to you the way they do. For example, they could be feeling stressed or ill. You may find it comforting to think about other reasons that could explain another person's behavior. For example, you might assume your partner is angry when he comes home and bangs on the door. There may be other reasons he shut the door. Work may be one of them.

Someone may say or do something that isn't directed at you but is intended to criticize or harm you. For example, "You are trying to irritate me by stirring my tea this way." You might be more aware that you may be sensitive, suspicious, or defensive when you become hypomanic or manic.

There are other reasons people behave the way they do. You may also take personal credit for events that have nothing or little to do with you, such as 'My team won because of me playing.' This can have embarrassing consequences and lead to manic grandiosity.

Fortune-telling

Fortune-telling is jumping to conclusions about future events.

This is when you believe your future projections will be true. This can be a common problem when you feel hopeless or anxious. It is important to look at other outcomes. This will help you realize that you cannot predict what the future will bring but can make positive changes. For example, fortune-telling is not an option if you study hard and are confident that you will pass.

Hypomanic thinking can lead to very optimistic thoughts. You can predict that whatever you do will be a success, even if you don't think about it. This unrealistic optimism leads to more risky and uncertain ventures. This is not realistic optimism.

You can be optimistic about something but not blind to the problems. Understanding the issues can help you make smart decisions, address them and adapt to circumstances that might not change. This will help you create a better tomorrow.

Hypomanic and manic thinking doesn't necessarily mean doom & gloom. You can challenge your thoughts and ideas when your mood is rising. However, this will help you see the positive and dangerous aspects of your thinking and take steps to improve your outlook and make better decisions for the future.

Blaming

Blaming is the tendency to conclude that you or someone else is to blame.

It is often only a small part of the story when someone is at fault for something. It would help if you looked for other contributing factors. You might say, "It's all my fault/your fault that the house isn't clean." But many factors contribute to the reason for the house not being clean.

It is possible to feel rushed into blaming and judging others.

Hypomania can occur without taking into account the contributing factors. Extreme thinking is a way to set high standards for others that you should meet. One example of an extreme should is: "You must always agree with my opinion, or you will not be my friend." This can also be accompanied by harsh labelings, such as "You are an idiot." or "You should always share my opinion." This can be reduced by looking at the whole person and considering the factors that lead to unrealistic expectations.

Overestimating the goodness and beauty of the world

Hypomanic thinking can lead to the assumption that others are trustworthy and supportive, without knowing their true nature. This can lead to unfavorable alliances. Sometimes it is better to dig deeper than just take the facts as they are.

It is easy to mistake feelings for facts

This is not about jumping to conclusions that you feel something.

It is the way it is. Although feelings are important, they shouldn't be confused with facts. It is not enough to feel something. It can be useful to step back and do a more objective assessment.

Over-generalizing

Over-generalizing involves reaching a sweeping negative conclusion.

Only a small portion of the evidence supports the assertions that there is a universal truth to everything and everyone. It is important to remember that not all evidence is the same. You might be wrong about other aspects of the situation. A bad situation does not necessarily mean that everything is bad. This can help identify the context of what went wrong. It can replace the phrase "I failed this assignment, so it means that I am ineffective and should give up" with "I failed this assignment, but I will still succeed the year. I will learn what went wrong to improve my next assignment."

Catastrophizing

Catastrophizing is about creating the worst possible scenario and then blowing it up.

Exaggerating the severity or consequences of a situation, such as rejection, suffering failure, or other seriousness, can increase your anxiety and hopelessness. Catastrophizing is when you use harsh language to describe the consequences. It is helpful to consider the possible less severe consequences and assess if there are realistic solutions. You could substitute the sentence "It's a disaster because I won't be able to find her home" with "It might be a nuisance if it's not possible to find her home as I may have to ask for directions." Sometimes people underestimate their abilities to handle problems and the difficult consequences. This can increase anxiety.

Labeling

Negative labels are like putting yourself and others under pressure.

You or they are placed in a box, so you can't notice any other characteristics or behavior. A stereotype is only one aspect of a person. Find a perspective that considers different parts of yourself and others.

Any other extenuating circumstances. You could also respond by saying, "You made a mistake, but you might do better next time," or "I'm not good at this particular thing, but I can do other things."

Insecure thinking

It is possible to form beliefs about your power, personal ability, and personality.

Attractiveness becomes more unrealistic the higher your mood goes. For example, "I can drive very quickly without an accident" or "I can pass this exam without any preparation." This thinking can cause you to think that you can achieve impossible goals or lead to dangerous or unrealistic consequences such as risky investments or sexual indiscretions. This can increase your activity levels and worsen your hypomania. To challenge these self-deprecating thoughts, you need to be realistic about your capabilities and not go astray.

LEARN MORE ABOUT MANAGING WORRIES

People with bipolar disorder can spend a lot more time worrying. While some anxiety can be helpful because it sends you a message to prepare for an event, constant worry could cause the opposite effect. Too much fear can make you lose your ability to concentrate and cause you to feel unsafe. It can also lead to a reluctance to do fulfilling activities, such as skipping a course to avoid anxiety about the exam. Worry can lead to the opposite of what we expect. Worrying can make it harder to live a happy life.

There are other ways to deal with difficult situations than worrying about them or trying to avoid them. Some tips, such as challenging anxious thoughts, learning effective coping skills, and reversing bodily changes. Psychotherapy can also be beneficial to you in managing your anxiety.

Anxious thinking can be challenging

Removing anxious thoughts about a situation can help reduce anxiety and catastrophizing. It is okay to accept that life is not always as planned. And that you can usually deal with the worst consequences and still live. It is often worse to anticipate than it is. It can be comforting to see concrete examples from your own life.

Effective coping skills are essential for survival. You can prepare yourself by understanding the situation and practicing coping skills. You could qualify for an exam or important meeting by considering how you handle different aspects. You don't have to be worried about unexpected difficulties. You can manage any problems by anticipating them.

Physical changes can be reversed

Relaxation techniques and other techniques that target the physiological changes that occur during anxiety may help calm you down.

HOW TO CHALLENGE NEGATIVE THINKING

Negative thinking can make you more likely to relapse when stressors happen. Sometimes, people find it helpful to challenge their negative thinking in stressful situations. This helps prevents them from becoming worse. A healthy lifestyle includes trying to keep a balanced view. These techniques can also help if you are experiencing residual symptoms, early warning signs, or symptoms of depression. It is easier to overcome depression if it is less deeply embedded.

REDUCING SUICIDE RISK FOR BLACK WOMEN

Suicide is not always a sign of mental illness. It can be precipitated by emotional distress or difficult life events. Suicidal ideation is mainly driven by hopelessness. People feel helpless when they believe that there is no way to succeed in the future. They lack hope, their future is dark, and they are not capable of happiness.

Female suicide rates

Although more women commit suicide yearly than men, black women are more at risk than any other race or ethnicity. The CDC states that black women are three times as likely to commit suicide than white women.

SIGNS OF SUICIDE-RISK

Sometimes, people get early warnings that they are at risk of suicide and take immediate action. For example, thoughts that life isn't worth living might be preceded by thoughts of self-harm. Other times, actual suicidal thoughts or impulses can be alarming.

You might notice warning signs such as mood symptoms or triggers or red alert signals that indicate imminent danger. There are ways to avoid suicide, no matter how early you recognize suicide risk. This can be made easier by recognizing early warning signs.

Triggers

For some people, certain triggers can cause them to consider suicide. This could be a conflict in a relationship, a loss of trust, social isolation, work pressure, too much alcohol, or drug abuse, particularly when combined with bipolar moods. These feelings can be reduced by finding ways to deal with them and getting better.

Other symptoms

Some signs may be similar to your warning signs, including hopelessness, withdrawal, and agitation.

You may experience mixed episodes or depressive symptoms. You can reduce your suicide risk by taking action before you feel suicidal.

It is especially important to recognize and share your hopelessness early. It is important to acknowledge and share your feelings of hopelessness. Also, it is important to challenge the negative thinking associated with this feeling. This will help prevent hopelessness from becoming overwhelming. It is easier to accept your hopelessness as a temporary symptom and not as a real reflection of reality.

Not only is it a warning sign of suicidal impulses, but it is also a warning sign that you are in danger. With all the pressures and emotions that come with an episode, it is possible to feel hopeless even after your symptoms have subsided. As your energy levels rise, the risk of suicide increases. To lessen your chances of committing suicide, you should allow sufficient time to get through this period. Once you have fully recovered, things will likely change for you. While your problems and difficulties may not have gone away, what has changed is that you can find solutions to the aspects of your life that you love and appreciate.

Danger signs

Talking about suicide is a good sign to share with others. You should also look out for symptoms such as resigning, giving up on commitments, writing letters about unfinished business or fixing your will. These signs could indicate that you feel suicidal or are planning to commit suicide.

You must take immediate action to lower the risk. Suicide plans are a sign of imminent danger. You need immediate help. Your risk of suicide is higher if you have ever attempted suicide.

A SUICIDE PREVENTION PLAN

Suicidal thoughts can sometimes feel all too real. It is difficult to recognize that it is a temporary symptom, not a serious illness. There are many other options for getting relief. It is important to develop strategies for managing your suicide risk while you are healthy. You can put your suicide risk prevention plan into action as soon as possible if you feel suicidal. To create such a plan, you need to consider what you and your family can do to lower your suicide risk. Below are some suggestions for how to prevent suicide.

What can you do to help?

If you feel suicidal, your safety should be a top priority. There are ways you can stay safe and get help. You can do things to help you get through this and decrease your feelings of suicidal thoughts or other mood symptoms.

- Tell your doctor about your thoughts of suicide.

- Book an emergency appointment if you have any questions or concerns.

- If you cannot reach your regular clinician, call your nearest hospital emergency department.

- You should remove all access to medication, pills, and car keys that could be used to harm you.

- Notify key friends and family that you feel suicidal.

- Keep in touch with others, so you don't feel alone.

- It is important to avoid alcohol and drugs.

- Talk it through with someone trusted or dial a suicide hotline

- Recognize that suicidal thoughts are temporary, and you don't have to accept them or act on them.

- Focus on the hour ahead. It is much easier to break down time when you are sick than to think about the future.

- You can make the difficult times easier to bear and help lift your mood. You can spend time with your loved ones, listen to music, write or play a musical instrument, pray, and do relaxation exercises.

- You can distract yourself from suicidal thoughts by going to the park, the mall, or the library.

- You might consider reaching out to spiritual or religious leaders or friends if you are interested in spirituality or religion.

Reduce symptoms

- Put your strategies to reduce relapse into action.

- Talk to your doctor about treatment. Certain medications can reduce agitation, anxiety, and impulsiveness, leading to suicidal thoughts.

- Find more positive perspectives by identifying your negative thoughts. The fact that you feel temporarily hopeless is not a sign of weakness does not necessarily mean that things are hopeless. It is possible to feel completely different about the future.

- Sometimes suicide isn't about dying but rather about trying to escape difficult situations. You can feel better about the future if you find new solutions to old problems. You can have a productive conversation with your clinician, a friend, or a relative about alternative solutions to old situations.

- Prioritize and delegate any stressful requests that cause you to feel overwhelmed.

- Ask yourself what could make a difference in your future. "It would make all the difference if my illness were under control," is one example. . "if I was in a relationship or. . . if I find something that I like to do, I will." Decide to work towards your goal and succeed in the meantime.

Make a list of Reasons to Live

You could develop a 'Reasons to Live List' when you are well and keep it in easy reach for the times when you feel suicidal. You don't need to include many items. The list can be kept short if you find them meaningful.

Examples include:

- You don't want your family, friends, or children devastated.

- You desire to see your children mature.

- You cannot leave the ones you love.

- It is your responsibility to live for those you love.

- The future could be different.

- You can change the future. Learn to adapt to your problems.

- You still have things to see and things to do.

- Suicidal thoughts are temporary signs of illness and cannot control your life.

- Many items are meaningful to you when you're well.

- You fear that your suicide attempt might fail and that you may be left with some scarring.

- It is not clear what will happen when you die.

- A mission or purpose is what you do need your life.

- It is important to be concerned about the opinions of others.

- There is hope.

What can others do for you?

Suicidality can be a serious symptom of illness. However, it is often taboo. Recent research found that only 49% of bipolar disorder patients who experienced suicidal thoughts had spoken with their doctor. It is possible to manage and control suicidal thoughts. This common symptom of bipolar disorder can also be addressed. Because they fear that the other person won't be able to help, some people hesitate to talk to their doctor, psychologist, or close friend about their despair or suicidal thoughts. They can help in many ways.

What your doctor can do

Your doctor can assess the severity of your situation and listen to you.

They can discuss your medications, risks and suggest appropriate treatment. They may require to see yourself more frequently to monitor your suicidal thoughts.

You can also talk to a psychologist about your thoughts and symptoms. They will suggest alternative methods of dealing with your distress and the contributing factors. If necessary, they will arrange hospitalization. You can get help from a psychologist and your strategies to alleviate your pain and prevent suicide.

How friends and family can help

Some people have close friends or family who can help them. If you are feeling suicidal, call them. These people can be helpful allies if you have them. You can also feel helpless and uninformed when you feel suicidal. You can talk to them about ways you could both be supported and what you can do to lower your suicide risk. These are some ways they could help you to develop positive coping strategies:

- Take away any weapons, medication, or other items that you believe could be lethal and store them temporarily. Also, discuss how they can help to make you feel safer.

- Spend time with you until your suicidal impulses stop.

- Listenin to you and trying their best to understand your feelings without being critical.

- Brainstorm with others to find solutions for difficult situations that seemed overwhelming. Also, set achievable goals that will make you feel optimistic about the future.

- Temporarily assist with heavy demands such as childcare

These suicidal thoughts are temporary. You may be able to see the future differently.

- You can distract yourself by doing things together like going on a drive or watching a film.

- Call your doctor or hospital emergency department and drive you to the hospital if necessary.

CHALLENGE EARLY THINKING

Cognitive-behavioral therapy teaches people to recognize, challenge, and replace unhelpful thoughts and behaviors, as we saw in the case of depression. This cognitive restructuring can be used with hypomanic thinking if you aren't too restless or agitated and still can consider other possibilities. Once you're completely manic, it is difficult to argue rationally with yourself.

This could reduce the chance of having negative consequences. You must be able to identify unrealistic thinking. You can learn how to use cognitive restructuring techniques to identify your hypomanic thinking patterns.

Recognizing your thought patterns and the typically helpful responses can help you disengage yourself from unhelpful habits. Cognitive restructuring should not be used alone to reduce your hypomania and mania prodromes. This strategy will help you change your relationship with hypomania, so you don't try to avoid it or pretend it isn't there.

As you ride the bipolar rollercoaster, there are a few ways that hypomanic thinking can be illogical or unhelpful. You may feel very strong emotions and judge others based on these feelings rather than examining the facts. Overly positive or negative thinking are early signs to look out for. You may have positive thoughts interspersed with negative thoughts. People with mixed mental states or dysphoric mania may have more negative reviews than others.

Hypomania can lead to early thinking changes such as a progressive increase in self-confidence and a focus on the immediate satisfaction of your needs or achieving your goals.

Overvaluing your goals and needs

Hypomania can lead to people becoming more focused.

They will get immediate satisfaction with their goals and needs. It could be the gratification of a desire, such as driving fast, purchasing a pair of shoes you cannot afford, or calling a friend at night. You may feel the need to do something, regardless of the impact on your health and the lives of others. A full episode of mania is when your desire for immediate satisfaction is stronger and more difficult to control. You may end up regretting the decisions you made. You can prevent some damage if you recognize this tendency early enough. These strategies will help you to do this without affecting your mood.

The world and others

It is possible to see yourself or believe that others see you in a very positive or negative light. These extremes could indicate that you are making assumptions and jumping to conclusions. These unrealistic thinking patterns are very common among other people.

The future

As optimism grows, people perceive situations as less risky and underestimate dangers for others.

Underestimating risks and consequences

Another side to this is the tendency to neglect the dangers of doing something that could have serious consequences. For example, "I bet my savings on a horse, but I'm sure it will win the race." Many people are guilty of underestimating the risks and consequences of being ill. This can lead to manic behavior. Although you can keep your thoughts in check and aren't too mad, it is important to recognize that you might be underestimating the potential negative consequences and real difficulties.

LIVING WELL

Recovery is the process of coming to terms and accepting your illness. It is "a deeply personal, unique process of changing one's attitudes, values, goals, skills, and roles." It's a way to live a fulfilling, hopeful, and productive life, despite limitations due to illness.

However, this term has been criticized because it implies that recovery is a final destination, a finite holy trinity. Talking about an illness that causes recurrent episodes or mild symptoms in between episodes can lead to the perception that recovery is a continuous process. For some, it may be easier than for others. Our view should be that coping with bipolar disorder can be described as a journey. It involves learning from trial and error how to manage your illness and make the most of your life.

The 'journey approach' is about active acceptance and coping. It involves taking control. This involves considering your bipolar disorder and your environment at that time and then using the appropriate strategies to help you maintain your wellness. Your approach to managing your illness will vary depending on its stage. For example, you might need to pay more attention to preventing relapses or improving in the hospital. Or, take things slow and not rush to finish your accumulated tasks after an episode. You may feel more able to concentrate on your future when you're well.

You can appreciate your personal qualities, talents, and values. This will help you live without being labeled and make it easier to enjoy your life.

It can help others to understand and relate to you and recognize when you are feeling isolated. When you're gregarious, manic, and shy at the same time, it can be hard to feel a consistent sense of who you are. When they are ill, people sometimes lose touch with their strengths and talents or what they value in life. It is easy to misinterpret your symptoms as who you are. Other people could fall for the same mistake. Self-stigma is perhaps the most effective form of stigma.

Self-stigma

When you believe in stigmatized labels, self-stigma can result.

You are a "mental patient," and you feel guilty about it. This is you. You accept yourself as you are, rather than seeing your bipolar disorder and illness as separate individuals. This allows you to get the opinions of others who don't understand your illness. It is the same when people think they are inferior because they have a particular religion or skin color. Stigmatization can severely affect your self-worth and make it difficult to recognize and express your strengths and talents. Your identity is constrained by living according to a label. Your illness may place restrictions on your life. For example, you might need to limit how social you engage to keep yourself well. However, self-stigma can increase the condition. Understanding your bipolar disorder and unique identity can help you overcome your prejudices.

Get to know you

Enjoy activities that make you feel good.

Harmony with your beliefs, values, and talents can help you feel fulfilled, even if your mood is not stable. This can be done by getting to know yourself, your illness, and what you have in your life.

It can be difficult to recognize your strengths and personal attributes. Some people are more aware of their limitations and faults. This is best done when you're well. Being depressed or elevated can cause your perspective to shift. Think about your skills and abilities in work, hobbies, sports, or daily life.

You may feel different from the person you were before bipolar disorder. While the illness can temporarily mask some people's talents and capabilities and limit what they can accomplish, it can also help them discover new skills and interests or use old ones in new ways.

Rebuilding

You may need to consider the following factors when rebuilding your life and yourself.

You can accept the limitations that your illness has placed on you and create a fulfilling life. This will allow you to set realistic goals and live a fulfilling and affirming life.

Bipolar disorder can affect everyone in different ways. While some people with bipolar disorder can continue to work while managing their illness, others have different ways of living and enjoying life. People with bipolar disorder usually make some adjustments to their lives.

Lifestyle changes are necessary to make the most of your life and keep you well.

External stigmatization

People with bipolar disorder are often confronted with prejudice, misconceptions, and discrimination. It is important to educate people about the differences between fear and misconceptions. However, attitudes towards mental illness are changing because of successful treatment, advocacy, and legislation. Effective treatment is the most important factor in decreasing stigma. People have more options when it comes to defending their rights.

Many say that expressing who they are through participation in life helps them see their illness better and gives them the confidence to make decisions if their rights have been violated.

To disclose or not?

Stigma is also linked to the decision to reveal your illness to others. It can be difficult to feel accepted and respected. This can lead you to avoid situations where your condition might be exposed. Some people may mix with others living with bipolar disorder to prevent stigma. Some people only tell trusted friends. Some people only disclose their illness to their boss or the human resources department at work. Others have 'come out of the closet' and declared their disease to the rest of the world. Some people have been more open about their bipolar disorder than others. This may have helped reduce misconceptions. You have to consider the pros and cons of disclosing your situation.

These choices might be easier as more accurate information replaces misinformation in the public realm. You may consider some things after you have assessed the situation and spoken with others in similar situations. Your view of yourself and your illness may be more than your illness. This will help others trust you and increase their understanding of your bipolar disorder. Depending on what the other person needs, how much information you will determine how much you share. You may choose not to use the term "bipolar disorder" in certain circumstances. In some cases, it might be appropriate to use "bipolar disorder" and provide more information. It is helpful to explain your bipolar disorder to those you care about.

Depending on your circumstances, you might include some or all of the following:

- A simple definition of bipolar disorder.

- It is a medical condition.

- There are effective treatments available. This means that you might have isolated episodes that can easily be controlled. You may also be mildly symptomatic in between episodes.

- You may appear the same person between episodes as they think you are. Only when you are symptomatic does your behavior change.

This explanation will explain how your work and relationships may temporarily affect your illness. There are many ways that someone can respond to symptoms of illness.

KEY POINTS

- Different people have different approaches to managing their bipolar disorder.

There are two extremes: rejecting it or actively seeking it out. They might live with their illness, limit their interaction with the outside world, or seek out highs to increase their depressive and manic episodes.

- It is common to deny your bipolar disorder, especially when it is first diagnosed. It can become problematic if you cannot manage your illness constructively because of denial.

- It may take some time to accept your bipolar disorder. Some people also go through grief, which can recur at different times.

- Accepting your bipolar disorder and continuing treatment can be difficult. However, it is possible to create a life and identity that you love within the limitations of your illness. This ongoing process requires you to adapt to your disease in different phases and make the most of it daily.

- Understanding your strengths, talents and values will help you see past the stigma of mental illness and stand up for your rights.

- You can decide whether or not to reveal your illness and what information you will give in particular circumstances.

CONCLUSION

Bipolar II can be a condition that people living with manic-depressive psychosis may develop. Many of the things we see today can be attributed to bipolar disorder in black women. This is because many black women with these mental conditions are not diagnosed with mood disorders like major depression or hypomania.

Black women are more likely to experience trauma in childhood and adulthood than white women. It is, therefore, interesting to see that black women are more likely to develop Bipolar II than white females. Research has shown that black women who have experienced childhood trauma are more likely to develop Bipolar II than black women who have not suffered from it. These studies also showed that Bipolar II is more likely for those with male relatives who have bipolar symptoms

This suggests that mental illness diagnoses should not be limited to symptoms but also include family history, gender, and race.

REFERENCE

Gitlin, M. (2020, January 28). *The existential crisis of bipolar II disorder - International Journal of Bipolar Disorders*. SpringerOpen. https://journalbipolardisorders.springeropen.com/articles/10.1186/s40345-019-0175-7

Hennig, S. (2018, November 29). *What It's Like to Be a Black Woman with Bipolar Disorder*. Maternal Mental Health Research Collaborative. https://research4moms.com/2018/03/15/black-woman-with-bipolar-disorder/

Hoffman, M. (2008, May 14). *An Overview of Bipolar II Disorder*. WebMD. https://www.webmd.com/bipolar-disorder/guide/bipolar-2-disorder#:%7E:text=of%20Bipolar%20Disorder%3F-,What%20Is%20Bipolar%20II%20Disorder%3F,never%20reach%20full%2Dblown%20mania.

Martin Richards, E. (2022, March 22). *Mental Health Among African American Women*. Johns Hopkins Medicine. https://www.google.com/amp/s/www.hopkinsmedicine.org/health/wellness-and-prevention/mental-health-among-african-american-women%3Famp%3Dtrue

Mary Soliman, PharmDPGY-1 Pharmacy Practice ResidentTallahassee Memorial Health CareTallahassee, Florida Soheyla Mahdavian, PharmDAssistant Professor for Pharmacy PracticeFlorida A&M University College of Pharmacy and Pharmaceutical SciencesTallahassee, Florida Marlon Honeywell, PharmDInterim Associate Dean for Academic Affairs and ProfessorFlorida A&M University College of Pharmacy and Pharmaceutical SciencesTallahassee, Florida Tiffany Welch, PABond Community Health CenterTallahassee, Florida. (2011, November 16). *Bipolar II Disorder in Adults: A Review of Management Options*. U.S. Pharmacist. https://www.uspharmacist.com/article/bipolar-ii-disorder-in-adults-a-review-of-management-options

Psychiatry.org - What Are Bipolar Disorders? (n.d.). American Psychiatric Association. https://psychiatry.org/patients-families/bipolar-disorders/what-are-bipolar-disorders

NOTES

NOTES